INTRODUCTORY
SOCIOLOGY

CLEP* Test Study Guide

© 2022 Breely Crush Publishing, LLC

*CLEP is a registered trademark of the College Entrance Examination Board which does not endorse this book.

971010221143

Published by Breely Crush Publishing, LLC
10808 River Front Parkway
South Jordan, UT 84095
www.breelycrushpublishing.com

ISBN-10: 1-61433-643-1
ISBN-13: 978-1-61433-643-3

Printed and bound in the United States of America.

Table of Contents

 What is Sociology?

Sociology is the study of people and their actions and how they relate to society. It's the science of how and why we have certain values, relationships, religion, etc. Sociology is about culture, beliefs, norms, values and attitudes. It is a study of art and language as well. Sociology also deals with social problems like homelessness, racism, etc. Sociologists, unlike psychologists, do not study motivation. Human behavior is studied by analyzing social interaction and grouping.

Auguste Comte is considered the Father of Sociology.

Max Weber

Max Weber was a German sociologist who proposed a theory of characteristics of efficient and effective bureaucracies. One of these characteristics was a hierarchical structure. This involved a specific command structure with a central decision making element. Another characteristic was divisions of labor. Weber believed there needed to be specific responsibilities in specific areas, with everyone specializing in a specific area. Third, he believed there needed to be specific and formal rule systems. According to Weber, rules needed to be specific, clearly defined, and easily understood.

Another characteristic stated by Weber was that bureaucracy needed to be deliberately impersonal. Often he applied this to the idea of property. The office's things belonged to the office, and the employee's things belonged to the employee. Because Weber's definition of a bureaucratic system depends on specialization, another characteristic is that employees should be selected on a basis of qualification. The final characteristic was the need for clear goals and purposes.

Max Weber was an economist and a sociologist. His three dimensions of social stratification are:

- Status
- Class
- Party (political)

He also linked the creation of capitalism to the Calvinist doctrine. Specifically, the doctrine of predestation. Predestation means that before you were born, God or a higher power "meant" or "intended" for you to do something.

Weber also believed in **legal-rational** authority that meant there were clearly defined rights and laws that must be upheld. His principle of **verstehen** explains how beliefs make people act.

Economic Institutions

The economy is a technical and official name for the production, distributions for goods and services in exchange for other services or money. When someone creates a product they in turn market and sell that product to a customer. This is the most basic activity in the economy. Currency is the most common way to purchase goods and services. Although barter or trade still happens, most transactions are conducted with currency or credit.

Macrosociology is when sociologists study large social institutions such as marriage or religion as a whole. **Microsociology** is when sociologists study social interactions on a smaller level such as on an individual basis.

Capitalism is a monetary and social system where individuals are encouraged to make new businesses and work for as great of a profit as they can. The United States is a capitalistic society. In a capitalistic society, the government has limited influence in private business although they do enforce some business laws and practices.

Socialism is a system where the good of the group supercedes the good of the private individual. Each person works for bettering society as whole. The government controls almost all natural resources, business and social programs.

In welfare capitalism, the government pays for all education and health coverage. It is a market based system as well. Sweden and Canada are examples of welfare capitalism.

Communism is when the means of production are owned equally and the profits are shared equally. Although it has been attempted many times to create a utopia of sorts based on communism, it is considered a flawed system. The book "Animal Farm" is a wonderful analogy to the social systems, particularly communism.

Globalization is the takeover and expansion of current markets into new global markets. For example, the cell phone market is still booming in the United States and has experienced great success in South America and other localities where the standard of living has been increased to allow for such products. Telecommunications are being added to the most rural of areas in South American and Africa. By searching out customers in these far places, companies are reaching new untapped markets of customers.

Two types of economic conditions are monopolies and oligopolies. In a monopoly, one business or company is the only place which sells or provides a particular product or service for which there is no substitute. Traditionally, monopolies are considered dangerous because it allows the business to charge whatever they wish for the product or service. For example, if there was only one gas station chain in the world, they could raise the prices on gas and people would have no choice but to pay.

Oligopolies are similar to monopolies, but different because instead of one business supplying the product, a few companies sell it, and because those few companies are so powerful, their policies influence and determine the actions of other business and each other. For example, think about the cell phone industry. Many large companies tend to buy each other out and merge, meaning that there are fewer and fewer companies. The ones that exist are quite large, with the small companies unable to keep up with the competition and go out of business.

The resource mobilization theory explains social movements as an attempt by people to join together in a rational manner to mobilize and obtain resources or reach goals. According to the resource mobilization theory, every social movement starts as an organization. That organization must then acquire support and resources, which it then uses in achieving goals. This theory applies to both political and economic situations.

Educational Institutions

Education is an important part of society. Education is more than just teaching reading and writing, although those are very important skills. Education and school is also a net for other social problems including learning disabilities, physical abuse, sight and hearing problems, speech problems, social problems, etc.

It is a well known fact that those people who complete high school will receive a higher paying job than those that do not. Those people that have a college degree will receive higher compensation than those with just a high school degree and so on. Basically, the more education you have, the better chance of receiving higher earnings.

Private school versus public school has been debated in several political arenas. In theory, the better the economic status of the area, the better the school, whether it be public or private. That said, the poor believe that they are disadvantaged because they will not receive as high of a quality education as a student attending private school. While this can be true, it is offset by the many opportunities for all people to information and education through the internet and public libraries. Scholarships are also available to students from an economically disadvantaged background.

Family Institutions

Family is an important part of culture and life. Family provides more than the other members in a family photo and the sharing of chores. As an institution, the family has important functions which include caring for children, to give membership and a sense of belonging and to transfer culture and traditions between generations.

The traditional family is also called a nuclear family which includes a mother, father and children living together. An extended family includes the nuclear family and grandparents, aunts, uncles, cousins, grandparents, etc. In older times and less modern societies, entire extended families lived in one house or one village. Now, many things such as college, new jobs and other opportunities drift families farther apart, at least geographically.

Occasionally, the classification non-family household is used to describe single person households with no children. An example of this would be a college student living in a dorm. Families can also be classified by dominance. In a patriarchal family, the father is the head of the household or dominant parent. In the United States, this is traditionally the case. Families can also be matriarchal, which is the opposite of patriarchal. In a matriarchal family, the mother is the dominant parent, for example, in the situation of a single mother. In an egalitarian family, the mother and father share authority.

The family institution is based on the institution of marriage. Although not apparent in all cultures, the following are the sociological definitions regarding the different types of marriage:

- Endogamy is when members of the same class or group marry.
- Exogamy is when members of different classes or groups marry.
- Monogamy is when one man and one woman marry.
- Polygamy is when one man marries more than one woman.
- Polyandry is when one woman marries more than one man.
- Matrilocality is when the newly married couple lives with the wife's family.
- Patriolocality is when the newly married couple lives with the husband's family.

Alternative families or blended families include step-parents, step-children and single parent households.

One question which faces newly married couples is where they will live. Societal expectations, in addition to person preferences, have great influence on such decisions. In a patrilocal society, it is expected that the son will bring his wife to his family's house, and she will move in with them. In a matrilocal society, it is expected that the husband will move in with his wife's family. In a neolocal society it is expected that the two will move to a neutral location, such as an apartment.

The terms matrilineal, patrilineal, and bilineal are used to describe the relationship to family after marriage. In a patrilineal society, the wife becomes a part of her husband's family. For example, societies in which the wife changes her last name to match her husband's, are societies which are patrilocal. In a matrilineal society, the husband becomes part of his wife's family after marriage. Often, matrilineal societies are also matrilocal. Bilineal societies are societies in which both the wife's and husband's family are equally important.

Medical Institutions

In each culture, the medical institutions differ. As Western medicine has evolved, the positions that originally treated conditions were dismissed as unscientific. However, there has been a recent surge in these older methods which include herbology, acupuncture and midwifery. The interest in these alternative forms of medicine are generally sought when people become unhappy with the results (or lack of) from Western Medicine.

Political Institutions

There are many types of government institutions. **Monarchy** is the political system is when one major family controls the government. The power passes from generation to generation. Swaziland still practices this type of government. Monarchy is best known for its positions of kings and queens. This is called absolute monarchy, when the king or queen has absolute control. Most common is a constitutional monarchy where the king or queen is symbolic but the elected officials actually do the work and politics. England is a great example of a **constitutional monarchy**.

Democracy is the form of government where the citizens elect their officials. The Unites States is a democracy. The United States is a two-party system. There are two parties, the Democratic Party and the Republican Party. The Democratic Party believes that the government should be active in promoting welfare of the country. The Republican Party believes that the government should be limited in providing social services.

Authoritarianism is a type of government which does not allow its citizens to participate in their government. China is an example of an authoritarianism government.

Totalitarianism is a type of government where the government controls almost every aspects of their citizen's lives.

Religious Institutions

Religion is a way to understand the reasoning of why things happen, including birth and death. Some scientists believe that religion is simply a tool to give or receive comfort in times of need. There are two types of religions. Religions based on a single deity or God are monotheistic and religions based on more than one deity or God are polytheistic.

There are several main religions in the world. They include:

- Christianity – Christians believe that Jesus Christ was the son of God and the savior of mankind. There are many variations of this belief and many denominations.

- Judaism – Judaism was around before Christianity. Jews believe they are the chosen people of God.

- Islam – People who believe in Islam are called Muslims. Muslims believe that the word of God was revealed to their prophet Muhammad. Although their God is referred to as Allah it is the same God that the Christians and Jews worship. Their sacred text is called the Koran.

- Hinduism – Hinduism is the oldest world religion. Hindus do not worship a specific God but instead believe in Karma, good works done will reward you, evil deeds done will harm you. They also believe in reincarnation which is when the soul is rebirthed.

- Buddhism – Buddhists follow Siddhartha Gautama from the sixth century. Their teachings include rejecting materialism.

In all of these religions there are different organizations. A church is a religious group that is accepted and part of society. For example, the Catholic Church is an example of a church. A sect is a religious group that sets itself apart from society in mannerisms as well as location. For example, the Pennsylvania Dutch or Amish are a sect. They choose to live a different lifestyle than others in the world, dressing differently and living without modern interference. In all religions in society there are those groups or individuals who are fundamentalists. This is simply a way of saying they are stricter in their interpretation of their beliefs. For example, they may be against liquor, smoking or doing work on Sunday.

A **cult** is a group that is outside all cultural norms. A cult leader is very charismatic and exerts extreme control and influence over a group. A cult will often surround members night and day with other members by using compounds to group living. Also, cult members are isolated from other friends and family to be "brainwashed". There have been many instances of family members forcibly removing their family members from cults, theoretically kidnapping them to perform an intervention. There have also been mass suicides of entire cults, the most famous being The People's Temple. This suicide involved the members drinking Kool-aid or grapejuice laced with cyanide and other drugs. It also appears that those unwilling to participate were shot or forcibly injected. The leaders of these cults are unbalanced and paranoid.

 # *The Beginning of Slavery*

Many people believe that slavery began in the New World. However, this is incorrect. Slavery has been around since the Bible was written. Slaves were taken as prisoners of war, for debts they owned and for payment for a crime that someone in their family may have committed.

The Portuguese were the first to import black slaves into the New World. They began with sugar plantations and then moved many more into mining for gold and silver.

Spain, England, Holland and France all participated in the buying and selling of slaves.

The **Triangular Trade** was known as shipping lines that connected Europe, Africa and the America's with slaves. Slaves were also forced to endure a "seasoning" process where they were prepared for sale. About 30% of slaves died during this seasoning process.

Location	Exports
Africa	Slaves
West Indies	Sugar, Molasses & Rum
England	Manufactured Goods
American Colonies	Fish, Grain, Flour & Lumber

All colonies had legalized slavery by 1750. Rising wages for indentured servants made slaves popular. Colonies developed laws to keep slaves under control. They restricted slaves of:

- Right to assembly
- Earning money
- Seek after an education
- Autonomy of movement

Many unspeakable acts were legal to perform on slaves under certain circumstances. The white colonists feared a slave revolt. Their livelihood depended on the willing or unwilling work of their slaves. Two slave revolts, one in South Carolina and one in New York, made slave owners more anxious than ever before.

Some colonists used black indentured servants. These servants were not slaves but had pledged to work for an individual for a certain amount of time, usually seven years, in exchange for being brought to the new world. These servants became the first Africans in North America. Slaves were in the lowest social class anywhere. Slavery still exists today in many different countries. One area that has gotten media attention is the sex slave trade prevalent in Asia.

Research

To study the way that people grow, learn, adapt and interact with others, psychologists use a standardized method so that other people in the scientific community can understand their findings and agree on research.

Scientists use a specific vocabulary to conduct their research. A **participant** is a person that a scientist studies in their experiment. They can also be referred to as a subject. When a scientist is performing an experiment on an animal, they are also referred to as a subject or a participant.

When scientists want to study an entire city, culture, or population, they will use a sample. A **sample** is a small collection of subjects. The number of people you need to participate to make the sample the most accurate is statistically generated based on the amount of the population.

Everything that a scientist measures and studies is called a **variable**. For example, if you were conducting research on insomnia, you would have variables which include the amount of time it takes a person to fall asleep, how much caffeine they ingest, how much alcohol or drugs they ingest, what distractions are in the room, etc.

Research must meet four main tests:

1. Research must be **replicable**. Another scientist, given the information regarding the experiment, should be able to reproduce the experiment with the same results. This is how the scientific community accepts or rejects new theories. If the experiment can be reproduced several times by different people in different organizations or locations, it lends to its credibility. This means that the theory must be quantitative, or measurable and not qualitative. Qualitative means that something is similar in structure or organization but it cannot be measured in numerical terms.

2. The research must be **falsifiable**. This means that a theory has to be stated in a way that can be rejected or accepted. Think of it as asking a yes or no question. Is smoking bad for you? The answer is yes or no, and can be proven. This could be stated as "smoking is bad for you because it contains carcinogens". This is a falsifiable statement. It needs to be stated this way so that it can be proved or disproved. If a researcher does not consider all the evidence, but ignores the information that does not prove their theory and accepts the information that proves it, they are showing **confirmation bias**.

3. The research must be precisely stated and conducted. A theory needs to be stated precisely so it can be replicated. Scientists use operational definitions to state exactly how a variable will be measured. For example, a researcher studying birth order may notice that children who are the oldest of several siblings tend to be more responsible as adults and parents. The researcher may conclude that this is because they have experienced more time nurturing and caring for younger siblings. In our birth order study, the scientist needs to find a way to measure responsible. He or she might decide that they will use the individual's credit reports as an operational variable to show responsibility.

4. Researchers must use the most logical, simplest explanation possible as an answer to their theory. This is also called the **principle of parsimony** or **Occam's razor**.

THE SCIENTIFIC METHOD

The Scientific Method is the accepted way to conduct research.

It contains several steps. First, a researcher created a hypothesis. This is the testable idea. Second, information is gathered through an experiment or research. This information either proves or disproves the theory which leads to the third step, refining the theory. At this point, it may be necessary to start the experiment all over, having applied the new information learned in the experiment. The fourth and final stage is developing a theory. Again, at this point, it is necessary to test the theory through the scientific method. Once a theory has been proved successfully by reputable researchers, the more times it is reproduced, the more credibility it has.

RESEARCH METHODS

Information for a theory or experiment can be gathered several ways.

Case Study

In a case study, a single individual (subject) is intensely studied. The researcher gets data through personal interviews with the subject, its employees, neighbors, contacts, etc., and by reviewing documentation or records (i.e., medical history, family life, etc.). Other sources for information are testing and direct observation of the subject.

Survey

A survey is a great way to get information about a specific type of information. For example, a survey would work well to measure performance in an office environment. These can be aggregated and used to improve employee performance. Usually with a survey, questionnaires are given out to participants who are then asked to answer questions to the best of their ability. When a participant fills out a survey themselves *about* themselves, it is called self-report data. This information can possibly not be as reliable as other research methods because subjects may be dishonest with their answers. For example, the question "Are you ever late to work?" may have respondents answering "no" when in fact, they are late but either do not remember that or are dishonest to avoid punishment or negative information about themselves. Many give the answers they feel that researchers (or themselves) want to hear instead of the truth.

Naturalistic Observation

Jean Piaget extensively used natural observation to study children. Naturalistic observation is when a researcher observes and studies subjects without interacting or interfering with them. Piaget observed the behavior of children playing in the schoolyard to assess developmental stages. Another example well known to television viewers of the series "Star Trek" involves "The Prime Directive". This is the most perfect version demonstrated (in fiction) of naturalistic observation. In the show, the researchers had the ability to view and study human cultures without being known to the subjects because of their advancements in technology. In the series, it was a great violation to interact with and impact the development of these cultures and societies.

Laboratory Observation

Laboratory observation is conducted in a laboratory environment. This method is selected to monitor specific biological changes in individuals. In a lab setting, expensive and sophisticated machinery can be used to study the participants. Sometimes one-way mirrors are used to observe the participants.

Psychological Tests

Psychological tests give information about participants. Some of the more common include standardized tests such as the Minnesota Multiphasic Personality Inventory also known as the MMPI (a personality test), aptitudes, interests, etc. A participant's score is then compared to the norms for that test. A test is valid if it measures what it is supposed to. For example, a test on depression will be able to measure a person's depression. If it cannot, then the test is not valid. Content validity is applied when a test measures something with more that one facet. For example, a test for overall cooking skills would not be valid if it only tested baking cakes and not other skills such as grilling meat or making soup.

Cross Sectional Studies

When people of different ages are studied at one particular time it is called a cross sectional study, because you have a cross section of the population or demographic that you want to study.

Triangulation

As a research method, triangulation involves validating data and claims by cross checking it with more than two sources. This can be done in a number of ways. For example, gathering data through three different methods, having an experiment conducted by three separate scientists, or proving something through three different methods.

Longitudinal Studies

Longitudinal studies are when people are followed and studied over a long period of time and checked up on at certain points. These are best used to study the development of certain traits and track health issues. An example of a longitudinal study would be: 600 infants that were put up for adoption were tracked for several years. Some infants were adopted, some returned to the birth mothers and some were put into foster care. Which group adjusted the best and why? Lewis Terman did a longitudinal study of smart kids. The results are that the children are happy adults.

Correlation Research

Correlation research is used to show links between events, people, actions, behaviors, etc. Correlation research does not determine the causes of behavior but is linked to statistics. Causation is the cause of something. Correlation is not causation. This is an example of FAULTY, incorrect causation: a child eats an ice cream three times a week. This child scores well on school aptitude tests. It is determined that eating ice cream will make you smarter and do better on tests. There are additional factors or many others including socioeconomic status resulting from educated parents who genetically pass on their aptitude for school as well as their influence on the importance of school. In this situation, it is most likely the parents who contribute to the child's aptitude scores.

When conducting a survey and you have completed compiling the data, you will be able to measure the correlation between certain traits and variables tested. A correlation coefficient measures the strength between the two variables. A correlation coefficient is a number between -1 and +1.

A **positive correlation** means that when one variable increases, the other variable increases as well. For example, the more a couple fights, the more likely they are to get a divorce.

When one variable increases and the other variable decreases it is called a **negative correlation.** An example of this would be babies that are held by their caregivers tend to cry less. When the amount of time they are held goes up, the time they cry goes down.

The higher the number of the correlation coefficient, the stronger the correlation. A +0.9 or -0.9 shows a very strong correlation because the number is closest to a whole positive number 1 or a whole negative number 1. A weak correlation is a +0.1 or a -0.1. A correlation of zero shows that there is no relationship between variables.

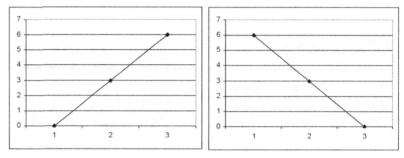

Positive correlation   Negative correlation

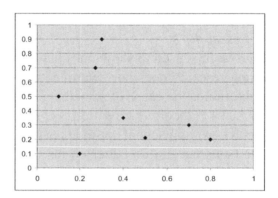

No correlation (above)

Census

A census is a collection of data from all cases or people in the chosen set. Usually, the most common form of a census would take place within an entire school or state. This means that every person of that school or state must be included. Censuses are usually not performed because they are so expensive. A census is valuable because it gives an accurate representation. To save time and money, survey companies will ask 1000 people or so (remember, the number changes based on the amount of people to be surveyed. A good rule of thumb is 10%). This is called sampling. For example, a recent census shows that the single person is the fastest-growing household type. So basically, a sample is a set of cases of people randomly chosen from a large group. The sample is to represent the group. The larger the sample, the more accurate the results.

READING CHARTS AND GRAPHS

Charts and graphs are easy ways to display information and make it easily readable.

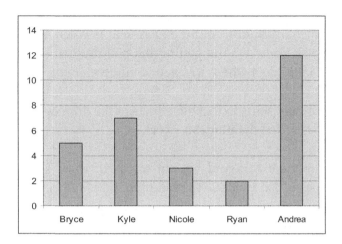

The above is a bar chart which shows five student's hours per week that they practice the piano. Are you able to tell who has the most hours and who has the least? How many hours per week does Nicole practice?

Name	Hours Per Week
Andrea	12
Bryce	5
Kyle	7
Nicole	3
Ryan	2

EXPERIMENTS

In experiments, a researcher manipulates variables to test theories and conclusions. Each experiment has independent and dependent variables. This is how researchers test cause and effect links and relationships.

The independent variable is the variable that researchers have direct control over. The dependent variable is then observed by the researcher.

In experiments, there are usually two groups of participants. One group is the experimental group and one group is the control group. The most common example is in medical trials. Let's say there is a trial run of a new diet drug. The researcher will split the group randomly in two. Group 1 will receive the diet pill that is being tested. Group

2 will receive a placebo pill. The placebo pill is simply a sugar pill. Group 2 will not know that they are not receiving the real drug. This allows the researchers to study the true effectiveness and side-effects of the pill. When the people are assigned to a group randomly, it is called **random assignment**. This particular experiment was a single-blind experiment. A **double-blind** experiment is when none of the doctors, researches and participants know who is getting the real drug. It is assigned by computer or an independent individual where it is kept confidential until the conclusion of the study.

When a participant starts to feel the effects of the drug but is *actually* taking a sugar pill or placebo it is called the **placebo effect**.

It is very important to avoid bias in research. Bias is the distortion of the results. Common types of bias include the sampling bias, subject bias and researcher bias. The placebo effect is an example of subject bias. Experimenter or researcher bias is avoided by conducting a double-blind experiment.

There are some disadvantages to experiments. They cannot be used to study everything. There are officially defined rules how humans and animals must be treated with the experiment. In an infamous experiment by psychologist Stanley Milgram, subjects were told that they were giving painful electric shocks to other people when in reality they were not. Some people consider this experiment unethical because it caused the participants emotional discomfort.

Researchers must get consent from their participants before conducting experiment. Informed consent means that the participants must know the content of the experiment and be warned of any risk or harm.

The **independent variable** in a study is the researchers have direct control over. Dependent variables are all other variables. The higher the correlation between the two factors is, the more closely the movement of one effects the movement of others.

Quantitative is a term used in research. It is used to describe something measurable, usually expressed as a number.

Qualitative is a term used to describe something similar in structure or organization.

Scientific Method is comprised of four steps:

1. Gather information

2. Generate hypothesis

3. Test hypothesis

4. Revise

   Mean, median and mode are three important terms in analyzing and understanding data. The mean of a set of data is also called the average, because it is one method of determining the average or normal value for a set of data. To find an average, add all of the numbers in a data set and divide the total by the total number of data. For example the average of 3, 4, 5, and 6 is 3+4+5+6 which equals 28 divided by 4 because there are four numbers. 28/4= 4.5. Therefore, the average is 4.5.

Another Example of Arithmetic Mean:

   What is the arithmetic mean of the numbers 10, 8, 6, 12, and 9?

   X = (10 + 8 + 6 + 12 + 9) = 45 and N = 5 because there 5 numbers in the list.

   Therefore, $\dfrac{X}{N} = \dfrac{76}{8} = \mathbf{9}$

   The mode is the number which occurs the most often. For example, the mode of the data set 3, 3, 4, 5, 6, 6, 6, 7, 8, 9, 9 is 6 because it is the only number which occurs three times.

For example, the Mode for the following set of data {10, 12, 14, 10, 8, 10, 7} is **10** because 10 appears the most number of times in the data set.

What is the "Median"? The Median is the middle value or the arithmetic mean of the middle values. The following example will demonstrate how to find the Median.

Sample Data = {3, 3, 5, 6, 7, 9, 10, 12, 14}

The Median = 7 because it has four numbers to the left of it and four numbers to the right of it in the sample data.

   NOTE: The data MUST be in numerical order to find the Median. For example, if you are given a sample data set of {5, 6, 12, 3, 3, 10, 7, 14, 9} you must first put it in numerical order: {3, 3, 5, 6, 7, 9, 10, 12, 14} to find the correct Median of 7.

Find the Median for the following set of numbers: {2, 3, 4, 5, 6, 7}

Since there is an even number of numbers in the data set you will need to find the arithmetic mean of the two middle numbers 4 & 5. (4+5)/2 = 4.5. Therefore, the Median is 4.5.

What is the "Range"? The Range is simply the difference between the largest data value and the smallest data value. For example, the Range in the set of {2, 4, 7, 8, 10, 12, 24} is 24-2 = **22.**

Conducting Research

An **aggregate** is a group of people that have accidentally or randomly come together to form a group. In sociology, a "group" is only made up of people that have social relations with each other.

A **primary group** is a social group with intense intimacy. The people in this group have strong social ties to each other. A good example would be a group of lifelong friends. They have years of experience with each other and shared interests and goals. They also usually inhibit strong personalities. The more homogenous a group is, the more likely they are to have interaction.

A **secondary group** is a less intimate group where people pursue the same goals but without a real sense of belonging. A good example of this might be your study group at school. Secondary analysis is doing research from anything that is not the direct source. This could include death certificates or other documented information like journals.

Social solidarity is the emotional intensity of the attachments in a group.

Social conflict is unfriendly interaction between groups.

The **independent variable** is one the researchers have direct control over. Dependent variables are all other variables.

Functional perspective is the idea that society is a system. People who study this perspective look for ways to see how it is operating.

Conflict perspective is when two elements in society are in conflict. There has to be some resolution in this conflict. This is what makes society go forward.

Causation is the principle that one variable affects another variable. The higher the correlation between the two factors is, the more closely the movement of one effects the movement of others.

Demographics

Demography or demographics is the study of human populations. Aspects such as population number, gender, race, education level, distribution, age, birth and death rates, income level, and lifestyles are just a few of the things that demographers study. This information is used by government agencies, businesses and researchers to make decisions. Demographics is an integral element of sociology, the study of societies.

By grouping people together, scientists can determine certain traits that people have in common. Those traits can then be studied further.

There are three basic ways in which people are classified. They are people are nationality, race, and ethnic group. **Nationality** refers to where a person geographically is, or what nation they are a citizen of. **Race** refers to a group which has common ancestors and inheritable traits, basically race is the biological category. **Ethnic group** refers to people who have the same culture. This can include anything from language and customs to eating habits. Often the three words are connected to each other. For example, people who live in the same nation will often have the same race or ethnic group. However, it is important to remember the distinctions between them.

Literally the word **fecundity** refers to the ability to reproduce. In the demographic sense however, it refers to the reproductive potential of a population. Essentially fecundity is a measure of how much of the population is physically capable of having children. This is generally considered to be women between the ages of 15 and 44.

Social Classes

Social classes are groups of the population which are divided based on wealth, occupation, power, or other qualities. Because of similar environments and experiences, people in the same social class often tend to share similar beliefs, customs or political beliefs. There are three different class groups.

The high class or upper class is at the top of the social scale. They are the most wealthy and powerful members of society. Below them is the middle class, which is comprised of people with stable jobs and a comfortable lifestyle. At the bottom of the social structure is the lower class. Members of this class have low or no income.

The social structure is also referred to as the social stratification. There are other systems of social stratification other than the class system, one of which is the caste system.

The caste system is based on inherited social status. In other words, if a person is born into a class, they stay in that class their whole lives. While class systems are broadly defined and allow social mobility, caste systems are rigidly defined and it is extremely rare for a person to change their caste.

Social mobility is classified in a number of different ways. Horizontal mobility describes a change in occupational position without a change in social status. For example, if a farmer changes what crop they grow, they have changed their occupational position, but their social status is still essentially the same. Another example is if a person changes jobs from working at a fast food restaurant to being a waiter at a nicer restaurant. Although they may have increased their pay, it is still horizontal mobility because they have not drastically changed their social status. Vertical mobility involves a change in social status. For example, if a person moves from being a factory worker to being a lawyer in a large firm. These horizontal or vertical changes can take place in a short period of time or over a long period of time. The ability for changes to occur within a single person's lifetime is referred to as intragenerational mobility. Changes which occur over multiple lifetimes are referred to as intergenerational mobility.

Culture Vocabulary

A society is a collection of individuals with common characteristics, such as distinct cultural, economic, or political systems. Societies can be described by their cultures. Culture describes a society's behaviors and actions. Some aspects which are included in culture are beliefs, customs, language, artistic styles, and values.

The main parts of culture are symbols, ideas, and objects that are created and used. **Society** is a self-sufficient group of people who live in a particular place and have social ties and relationships that hold them together. In that society, there is a social structure, which determines social roles. Those roles are learned throughout the life cycle.

Stratification is the unequal distribution of rewards (objects, money or other things perceived as valuable) between members of the society. The "higher" you are in society, the more you get.

Classes are groups of people who share a similar position in the stratification system. This means that the people at the "rung" of the society ladder mostly only associate with each other and not with those of lower classes.

Mobility either **upward mobility** or **downward mobility** means a change in the social system, sometimes by marriage. Someone from a lower class may be elevated through marriage to someone of a higher class. This means they have upward mobility.

Status is the rank or level of the person within the society.

Ascribed status is a position given to those who have not achieved things on their own but may be the child of the governor or the same race of those in authority (for example, whites in South Africa). Some other examples are: being 21, being white and being male. These are all ascribed statuses.

Achieved status is a position gained by achievement. A good example of this is Julius Caesar. He gained status through his accomplishments as a soldier.

Local networks are dense networks with strong and redundant ties. They are local networks because they engage in direct face-to-face interaction. A good example of this is an immediate family. There is a tie between the mother and father and from them to their children. The children also have ties to each other, some stronger than others and ties back to the parents. Those in local networks don't have to be families but they are clustered geographically.

Cosmopolitan networks are full of holes which are places where ties are weak. These networks are usually scattered geographically.

Values are ideals or standards about what is desirable in behavior.

Norms are rules that define expected behavior in particular circumstances. For example, in some families, it is expected that when you are invited to a family dinner you must bring your spouse and children. In addition, you must stay for after dinner games or dessert. Although those things were not literally included in the invitation, it is expected or you are considered rude.

Folkways are a set of manners and actions that are a part of everyday life in a society, like an American having a sandwich for lunch or someone in England having their afternoon tea.

Mores are customs that are very important to the culture.

A **law** is a rule created by the government.

Culture is the sum of all human creations, intellectual, through art, moral and physical. Culture is a complex pattern of living life in a society with certain rules. In time, some rules may be added or taken away.

A **role** is a set of expectations of a person's behavior based on their position in society. An example of this is that a mother has different responsibilities than the family pet. Subculture is a culture within a group that has its own set of beliefs, morals, values and norms, which must be adhered to. This sets the group apart from the surrounding society.

Prejudice is made up of negative attitudes and thoughts about a particular group.

Ethnocentrism is when a person thinks that everyone should be just like themselves.

Cultural relativism is when the meaning or significance of a trait or object depends on a cultural background. An example of cultural relativism is that in China they eat dogs where in the United States they are family pets. **Socialization is how a person learns how to live in his or her social environment.**

Gender socialization is showing the differences in the way boys and girls are socialized. For example, studies show that girls receive less attention from teachers than boys do.

Anti-Semitism is prejudice against Jews.

Anomie is the instability in a culture because of the erosion of morals.

Assimilation is the process by which a person takes material into their mind from the environment, which may mean changing the evidence of their senses to make it fit.

Accommodation is the difference made to one's mind or concepts by the process of assimilation. Note that assimilation and accommodation go together: you can't have one without the other.

A **normative order** is unique to human groups. It is a creation of standards. Where animals may have some social structures in leadership or territory, only humans actually have standards of conduct.

Merton's anomie theory says that deviance happens when people are blocked from achieving socially approved goals through legitimate ways.

The **looking glass self** is a person's self-concept (or self-esteem) based on how others see and treat them.

Dramaturgy is defined as the act of writing and producing plays, however it has a different meaning from the sociological perspective. In sociology, dramaturgy is a perspective which views behavior in terms of context instead of cause. In dramaturgical perspective, it is a person's situation or audience which determines how they act. In effect, every person's life is a play, which they write though their actions and choices. For example, a person may speak or act differently when they are with their friends than when they are with their grandparents.

Differential Association Theory

The differential association theory is a theory in criminology that describes why individuals become criminals. The theory was developed by Edwin Sutherland who claimed that crime is a behavior that is learned by association.

In other words, the more exposure and individual has to crime, then the more likely they are to become a criminal themselves. Sutherland developed nine points to describe the differential association theory.

Sutherland maintained that criminal behavior is learned behavior, not an inherent personality trait. He also claimed that such behavior is learned through communications with other individuals and by interacting with them. Sutherland felt that such learning typically happened in small, tight-knit groups. Through exposure and communication with criminals, an individual has the opportunity to learn how to commit the crimes in addition to coming to view it as socially acceptable or desirable to do so. This type of learning occurs similarly to any other type of learning, and becomes stronger with frequency, duration and intensity. Because crime is essentially a learned behavior it explains how criminals come from all walks of life - from those in poverty to white collar criminals in high-salary industries. The main criticism of Sutherland's theory is that it fails to account for individual personality differences which could predispose certain individuals to certain behaviors.

Folkways & Mores, Values & Attitudes

There are many different terms for classifying a person's beliefs or motivations. Why people do or feel the way they do? Some of these terms are attitudes, values, folkways, and mores. Attitudes are a person's general beliefs or opinions. A person can have many different attitudes, some of which are even contradictory. Values are more concrete and fundamental beliefs. Values are used when a person has conflicting attitudes they need to prioritize or choose between. For example, youth are often told to "have a better attitude," implying that it can be changed but they are also told to stick to their values.

Attitudes and values describe how a person reacts to or feels about a situation. Folkways and mores describe the effects of society. Folkways are expectations that, although they are not enforced, are practiced by societies. In other words, folkways are norms or expected behaviors. Table manners, for example, are a folkway. Mores are similar to folkways in that they are expected behaviors, but they deal more with moral issues, and are taken more seriously. For example, a society's beliefs about murder or kidnapping. A person who violates the mores of a society will face disgust and punishment, whereas a person who violates folkways faces milder reactions such as surprise. Laws are different from either of the two because they are rules, and therefore are specifically enforced, whereas folkways and mores are expectations.

Groups

In sociology, amalgamation occurs when two groups which were previously distinctly racial, or ethnic intermarry and create a new group. For example, when the Spanish conquered the people of South America, the Spanish men married with native women. Their children were given the name mestizos, a mix, or amalgamation, of the two races.

Assimilation refers to one individual or group changing or adapting to become like another. When someone assimilates into another culture, they adapt and are absorbed into it. Integration involves a compromise of sorts. Integration is when two individuals or groups combine or mix, with the result containing elements of each. Generally, the distinction between the two is that assimilation involves adaptation which is often seen as a loss of culture, while integration involves incorporating different elements of each.

Cultural pluralism refers to situations where smaller cultural groups are able to retain their cultural practices and are accepted by the community or wider culture. Simply put, cultural pluralism is when more than one culture exists in close proximity. For example, in the United States there are many different religions, all of which are accepted without discrimination.

Every day people associate themselves and interact with many different primary and secondary groups. A primary group is a small group of people who share opinions and hobbies, spend a lot of time together, and care about each other's well being. Primary groups require face to face contact and personal interaction. One way to think about it is that primary groups are like a person's close friends or family. Secondary groups are more formal groups that people identify themselves with. Although people in secondary groups may share a common interest, they have little contact with each other otherwise. For example, people who are members of the same clubs, or students who share a class. Secondary groups may develop into primary groups, but are usually well defined.

Endogamy is when people only marry within their own groups. For example, people marrying others from the same city. Another example of endogamy is the royal families of Europe, which became greatly inbred after hundreds of years of marriages between royals for political purposes. Exogamy is just the opposite. When people marry outside their own group or culture it is called exogamy. Endogamy and exogamy can apply to anything from race to political status.

Gameinschaft and Gesellschaft

The German sociologist Ferdinand Tonnies introduced the idea of gameinschaft and gesellschaft. Gameinschaft is a situation in which the condition of the group is considered as important as or more important than the individual. Tonnies believed that the family was the best example of gameinschaft. Gesellschaft is a situation in which the larger group is less important than the individual, who looks out for themselves. For example, in a factory the workers and management have completely different roles, and care little about the actual product. People work to make money for themselves.

Society and the Law

In 1954, the Supreme Court heard the case Brown v. Board of Education of Topeka. Prior to this historic case, many states and the District of Columbia operated racially segregated school systems under the authority of the Supreme Court's 1896 decision in Plessy v. Ferguson, which allowed segregation if facilities were equal. In 1951, Oliver Brown of Topeka, Kansas, challenged this "separate-but-equal" doctrine when he sued the city school board on behalf of his eight-year-old daughter. Brown wanted his daughter to attend the white school that was five blocks from their home, rather than the black school that was 21 blocks away. Finding the schools substantially equal, a federal court ruled against Brown.

Meanwhile, parents of other black children in South Carolina, Virginia, and Delaware filed similar lawsuits. Delaware's court found the black schools to be inferior to white schools and ordered black children to be transferred to white schools, but school officials appealed the decision to the Supreme Court.

The Court heard arguments from all these cases at the same time. The briefs filed by the black litigants included data and testimony from psychologists and social scientists who explained why they thought segregation was harmful to black children. In 1954, a unanimous Supreme Court found that "...in the field of education the doctrine of 'separate but equal' has no place," and ruled that segregation in public schools denies black children "the equal protection of the laws guaranteed in the Fourteenth Amendment."

In local law, prosecutors work to convict as many criminals as they can. Occasionally in a criminal case, the prosecutor will offer the defendant a plea bargain. There are two types of plea bargains. In a charge bargain the defendant agrees to plead guilty to a lesser charge or plead guilty to some of the charges against them. For example, if charged with drunk driving and driving without a license, they may plead guilty to only the drunk driving charge. The other type of plea bargain is sentence bargaining. This is when the defendant agrees to plead guilty for a shorter sentence. This way the prosecutor convicts them of the most serious charge, but they get less than the maximum jail time.

Karl Marx

Karl Marx lived in the nineteenth century, and although his name is often associated with communism, it existed before his theories were developed. However, Marxism did have a strong influence on communism. A result of the Industrial Revolution, which began in the eighteenth century, was widespread poverty which accompanied industrialization. Industrial workers across Europe worked dangerous jobs at low pay and in bad conditions. Marx saw this impoverishment as a direct result of capitalism. His most famous work, the Communist Manifesto, was published in 1848 and outlined Marxism. Marx believed that there were basically two social classes, which he termed the proletariat and the bourgeoisie.

The bourgeoisie was the privileged class with control of resources, or capital. The proletariat was the working class, whose only capital was their time. Marx believed that an inevitable side effect of capitalism was the exploitation of the proletariat by the bourgeoisie. Essentially, by paying the workers less then they deserved, the bourgeoisie was exploiting them, and this was the cause of poverty. According to Marx, this exploitation would eventually cause a collapse of capitalism, in which the proletariat would rise up in rebellion and create a classless society. This theory is known as Marx's conflict theory, because of the conflict between the classes, or class struggle, that occurs.

Marx also believed that the economy was the most basic institution followed by education, family, etc.

The term false consciousness is derived from Karl Marx's theories. False consciousness is the idea that the higher classes are misrepresented to the lower classes. The higher classes purposely portray themselves as dominant, and because of this the lower classes view themselves as subordinate. This is a false consciousness which stops them from seeing their potential for upward mobility.

Pluralist Model

The pluralist model is a theory that describes how power is distributed within a society. According to the pluralist model, power is fragmented and divided among many different groups. Although these groups do not represent a majority of the population, they do wield a significant amount of power. The groups are able to work with government in order to find solutions to problems and advocate for their concerns. However, because the power is broadly distributed among several groups, negotiation is necessary and often leads to outcomes and solutions that are fair and well-reasoned. Associations that are recognized as groups in the pluralist model include labor unions, political action committees, professional associations and so forth. Although power is not necessarily equally distributed between the various groups, it is fragmented such that no single group holds all the power.

The Power Elite

In 1956, Charles Wright Mills wrote his book *The Power Elite*, in which he discussed his power elite theory. The power elite theory divides the population into three groups, which can be organized into a sort of pyramid. The smallest and highest level, the power elite, is a small group of people who regularly decide the most important decisions for the whole country, as opposed to multiple groups who all work together to make decisions. The middle level deals with relatively minor issues, and the masses have no decision making power at all. For example, the President of the United States and his closest advisors and cabinet members would be members of the power elite, along with the most influential members of the legislature and the Supreme Court.

George Herbert Mead

George Herbert Mead was a sociologist born in the mid nineteenth century. He believed that both the mind and the "self" were products of social environments. According to Mead, the self was not present when a person was born, but develops through their social interactions and as they understand their relation to others in the society. Later, this concept came to be known as the social interactionist theory.

As people communicate and interact with others, their personal behavior is adjusted. Mead's concept of society requires the understanding that people are parts of a whole. Essentially, he believed that just like a foot is part of a body, a person is part of a society. While a body has and needs feet, a society requires individuals. The foot is not the whole body and a person will not be the whole society. Rather, each individual's part of society functions in their area.

George Herbert Mead was also known for his theories about the progression of children as they develop a self-identity. Mead believed that how individuals view themselves is based on the expectations and behaviors of those in their surroundings.

According to his theories, socialization is the lifelong process that an individual goes through as they develop their sense of self. The process begins in the preparatory stage. This is also known as the imitation stage because that is primarily what occurs here. This stage encompasses the first year or so of life in which a child can only imitate what they see being done around them.

This stage is followed by the play stage. In the play stage a child begins to connect the actions that they have been imitating with specific roles. They take on a mindset of role-playing the various actions that they have seen. For example, a child may pretend to be a chef, mother, firefighter, dancer, or anything else. In the play stage a child will take on only one role at a time. This stage lasts from approximately age 2 to age 6.

The final stage is the game stage. In this stage a child becomes capable of assimilating multiple roles. They begin to see the place of various roles in relation to others and become able to either involve several individuals in their role-plays or to assimilate several roles into a single game. These stages are known as Mead's three stages of self.

Christine Williams

Christine Williams is a professor of sociology at the University of Texas. She has written many books, including *Gender Differences at Work: Women and Men in Nontraditional Occupations*, *Still a Man's World: Men Who Do "Women's Work,"* and is the editor of *Doing 'Women's Work': Men in Nontraditional Occupations*. Her works are highly feminist and generally relate to women's rights and other gender related issues.

Second Shift

Arlie Russell Hochschild is known for her book *The Second Shift* that discusses the role of women in the workplace. Hochschild notes in her book that working mothers essentially have a second shift when they return from full time jobs. Their first shift is the paid full time job that to go to for the majority of the day. The second shift is the unpaid housework and childcare that must be provided once they return home. According to Hochschild, this second shift totals to approximately an extra month of work for the woman compared to her spouse. Hochschild advocates a restructuring of the workplace and of ideas about working women in order to be more accommodating to working mothers and growing families.

William J Goode

William J Goode wrote the book World Revolution and Family Patterns. In his book, he discussed how as industrialization occurs, the family patterns across the world have changed, and theorizes about how they will continue to change. He gathered data from various countries, including India, China, Japan, areas of Africa and the Middle East. One of his theories was that in developing countries, divorce rates would first fall, then rise. This seemed to be confirmed with the data that he gathered.

Double Consciousness

Double consciousness was a phenomenon first described by W.E.B. DuBois in his book *The Soul of Black Folk*. The concept of double consciousness describes the feeling of having more than one social identity. For DuBois this specifically referred to the difficulty of African American individuals trying to assimilate into the greater American culture. He felt that they were forced to see through two different lenses – that of an American and that of a black person. This can be applied to broader situations as well. Other races, social groups, disabled individuals, and so forth can experience the phenomenon of double consciousness. This inherently results in a sort of identity crisis for individuals experiencing it.

World Systems Theory

Immanuel Wallerstein is known for his work in developing world systems theory. This theory is a framework describing the development of the modern world, and describes the stages that occurred in making the world what it is today. According to Wallerstein, the world is one large capitalist market primarily influenced by availability of goods. Wallerstein divided the world into three different types of states: core, semi-periphery, and periphery. Peripheral areas are the underdeveloped nations. Due to their disadvantage in terms of development and industrialization they are exploited as a source of cheap labor and resources. The semi-peripheral areas are the "in between" areas. They having growing economies and marketplaces, but lack the sophistication of fully urbanized regions. Finally, the core regions are the most developed, urbanized, and industrialized states which hold geographic, economic, military, and educational advantages.

Social Institutions

Social institutions include many areas including religious institutions, the family, school, political systems, etc. The family is one of the most important. A social institution could be defined as a part of social life that is designed to meet important needs and support values. These include political organizations such as the Republican or Democratic Party. For example, the government supports schools through local property taxes.

What needs emphasis today is the political significance of the family. A people whose marriages and families are weak can have no solid institutions.
--**Michael Novak**

Why do we hear so much about the family nowadays? The stories seem to be either negative (i.e., stories of family violence and failures to properly care for their young and old, the breakdown thesis), reformative (e.g., the Christian Coalition's Contract for the American Family), or where have the "good old days" gone (i.e., federal statistics showing rising divorce rates, how three in ten births are illegitimate, or the disappearance of the Ward and June Cleaver family model) in tone. Perhaps all of the attention owes to shared assumptions that relationships between family members is the prototype for all other social relations, that the family unit is the fundamental building block for all societies, and that the family is society's shock-absorber of social change. One cannot, for instance, expect a person to do more for a stranger or an acquaintance than what he/she would do for a family member. And, as Michael Novak observes above, if the family breaks down not all of the remaining institutions can put "society" back together again.

WHAT IS "FAMILY"?

Preparations for the 1980 White House Conference on the Family collapsed when representatives of the political left insisted that the word "families" should be used instead of "family" to acknowledge the vast diversity of American family types. *Webster's Dictionary* offers twenty-two definitions. The Census Bureau defines a family as "two or more persons related by birth, marriage or adoption who reside in the same household"--a definition selected by only 22 percent of a random sample of 1,200 adults in a 1990 survey conducted by Massachusetts Mutual Insurance Company.

Is family ultimately based on blood--hence an adopted son is a lesser son, and a stepfamily is a lesser family? In 1993, a Florida teenager who had, upon her birth, been sent home with the wrong family, did not want to go to her biological parents when the mistake had been uncovered. In the legal case that resulted, her lawyer began with the question "What constitutes a family?" and claimed that "[biology] alone--without more--does not constitute or sustain a family."

Should the word be defined in terms of:

- those who live under the same roof, which basically means any household qualifies? A New Jersey court ruled that male college students sharing a renewable four-month lease fits the definition.

- the functions it performs? George Peter Murdock argues that the family is "a social group characterized by common residence, economic cooperation, and reproduction. ... [it] includes adults of both sexes, at least two of whom maintain a socially approved sexual relationship, and one or more children."

- legal recognitions of the relationships?

What difference does it make how "family" is defined? As will be developed, there are political, economic, legal, and religious interests bound up with the definition. Sociologically, being identified as a "family member" implies differences in the social rights and obligations toward others who are identified (both by the broader society and by the members, themselves) as "family" as opposed to being a stranger, colleague, neighbor, roommate, friend or one so distantly related (e.g., fifth cousin twice removed) as to not really "count" as family. (Of course, where a culture draws this line between family and not-family is highly variable; one is no more distantly related from any other person on earth than a fifty-second cousin or so. Pet owners and their pet owning friends may view Fido as "family"--and Fidos have been known to inherit the bulk of their deceased owners' estates.)

THE PERSONAL BENEFITS OF FAMILY LIFE

Despite controversies over what the "family" is, there is considerable evidence about what the consequences of family life are for individuals. For instance:

- Between 1973 and 1981, Yankelovich found that about three-fourths of Americans interviewed claim that family life was their most important value.

- Studies of the various life spheres Americans report as being sources of a "great deal of satisfaction" consistently show family life as being the most important

- Marriage increases life-expectancy by as much as five years. James Goodwin and his associates (*Journal of the American Medical Association* 258:3125-3130) found in their analyses of 25,000 cases listed in the New Mexico Tumor Registry, which tracks all malignancies in the state, a higher percentage of married people survive cancer at nearly every age.

- In Lewis Terman's famous longitudinal study of gifted California children (n=1,521), begun in 1921 with follow-ups every 5 or 10 years, it was found that those whose parents divorced faced a 33 percent greater risk of an earlier death (average age at death=76 years) than those whose parents remained married until the children reached age 21 (average age at death=80). According to Dr. Howard Friedman, who did the analyses, there was no such mortality effect for children whose parents had died (cited in Daniel Goleman. 1995. "75 Years Later, Study Is Still Tracking Geniuses." *New York Times* [March 7]).

 # Time

In the lifetime of one born in 1976, America's bicentennial year, the population of the world has increased by over one and one-half billion individuals, hundreds of thousands have died in the name of nationalism or religion, trillions of dollars have been spent perfecting doomsday weaponry, and the revolutions in minority, gender, and old age relations have shaken the traditional foundations of social life.

To make matters even more interesting, we are told that the pace of such change is accelerating. And with people living ever longer, the historical changes that used to be absorbed by several generations now must be coped with within a single lifetime. Largely forgotten are the principles and values on which society's oldest members based their lives. With the accelerating push forward generated by technological and scientific innovations, the future is supposedly coming closer. However, as a society, we seem unable to conceive of great enterprises--like the medieval construction of the great cathedrals of Europe--that can link generations together into a common project spanning several centuries.

Simultaneously, the past--the wake in the water produced by the bow of the future and the hull of the present--is growing longer, thanks to technology replacing personal memories: on celluloid for instance, we can see and hear George Bernard Shaw--a man born a decade before the outbreak of the American Civil War--talk to us about first hand experiences with the Victorian sexual mores. Ironically, the extent of our historical ignorance is considerable, and by all accounts growing.

This is the study of time and the various timetables and rhythms that shape our behaviors and thoughts. Here we will consider such issues as:

- the different meanings we give to each day of the week and months of the year.
- the "quality time" that working parents worry about sharing enough of with their children.
- the pressure we feel to be "on time" in the face of dreaded deadlines.

- the various social clocks whose tickings seem to govern our lives, such as the ages at which we believe we should be married, have children, or be "peaking" in our careers.

- our cultural fears of growing old and the meanings we give to the various stages of the life cycle.

- the emergence of "flexitime" and four-day weeks in the world of work.

- the types of time that religions impose to fortify the moralities of their members, such as eternity in heavens or hells, purgatory time, or escaping the cycle of death and rebirth.

- our sense of connection with generations long dead and those yet to be born, including such topics as time capsules, intergenerational contracts and legacies, ancestral worship, and futuristic themes in amusement parks and cinema.

- history, too, will be fair game--at least our interpretations of it. The past, after all, has passed, and its placement into the present is a social phenomenon that serves various social interests. Also of sociological relevance are individuals' perspectives of social change, for instance, whether they believe their countrymen to be happier or better off than they were twenty years earlier.

Time is the container of our social activities, especially in our monotonic culture where we have specific times for doing specific things (as opposed to more polychronic cultures, where many different things are done simultaneously). These time-specific activities flavor the meanings we associate with the various times of the day, week, and year. On the other hand, these time containers have a way of flavoring their activities as well. An evening college class, for instance, has an entirely different feeling than its daytime counterpart by virtue of the meanings and activities associated with night hours.

Even though these times of our lives seem to be as "natural" as any physical object in our social universe, the fact is that most are totally man-made notions. Why do we have 60 seconds in a minute and 60 minutes in an hour? Because the Babylonians had a counting system with a base of 60. Had the British had invented time with their base-10 system, we Americans undoubtedly would have hours made up of 100 minutes and minutes divided into 100 seconds. For that breed of social scientists known as temporal determinists, the big story is how the natural rhythms historically shaping these social times are being replaced by artificial tempos. And just as the meaning of a funeral dirge is altered when put to a calypso beat, so these new tempos have fundamentally altered the entire socio-cultural order. As a result, many people now find themselves feeling somehow "out of sync": out of sync with their bodies (i.e., "jet lag"), with their families and friends (i.e., the senses of not having enough time and time conflicts), and with the broader society (i.e., suffering "future shock"). Perhaps of all our taken-for-granted reifications that reveal "false consciousness," time is the most ubiquitous and "real."

Given our preoccupations with time, perhaps our species is better labeled *chronos sapiens*.

 Fertility Rates & Mortality Rates

A total fertility rate is the amount of children all women could have if they had children consecutively during all of their childbearing years. The total fertility rate is a more direct measure of the level of fertility than the crude birth rate, since it refers to births per woman. Here are the numbers for some selected countries:

Country	Rate
Afghanistan	5.72
Australia	1.77
China	1.82
France	1.72
Somalia	7.05
United States	2.07

Infant mortality rates refer to deaths of babies that are one year old or younger. **In the past 30 years the infant mortality rate in the U.S. has declined among both Caucasians and African Americans but remained twice as high for African Americans as compared to Caucasians.** Here are the rates for the same countries listed above:

Country	Rate
Afghanistan	144.76/per 1000 live births
Australia	4.9/per 1000 live births
China	27.25/per 1000 live births
France	4.41/per 1000 live births
Somalia	122.15/per 1000 live births
United States	6.69/per 1000 live births

There are variations between countries and their demographics. For example, the United States has the lowest percentage of women physicians in the world as well as a lower voting turnout than most European nations. Specifically, out of all the states in the U.S., Massachusetts has the highest number of physicians per 100,000 people. Comparing the U.S. population in general to Asian Americans in general shows that Asian Americans have more formal education and training.

Some statistical data is used to show health or the state of the economy. The economy of a given country can be broken up into different areas. Some of these areas are agricultural, industrial, public, service and information industries. The Industrial area is where raw materials like gold or lumber are removed from the area and processed into goods. Sometimes "cheap labor" is obtained by U.S. or other rich countries by exporting work to areas of the world where labor is less expensive than the U.S. (plus, there are less restrictions).

In the United States the number of women in the 85+ groups is nearly double the number of men of the same age. Generally, the reason for this is considered to be that men tend to participate in more dangerous activities. Statistically, men are involved in more car crashes, homicides and suicides than women are. Also, as medical technology has improved the likelihood of dying in child birth has greatly decreased, which heightens the average life expectancy for women.

Demographic Transition Theory

The demographic transition model was developed by an American demographer Warren Thompson. The model describes a transition by countries from a state of high birth and death rates to low birth and death rates as they become increasingly developed. There are four stages in the demographic transition model.

The first stage is that of pre-industrial societies. Due to low economic development in these areas, medical practices are primitive and infant mortality is high. This keeps the population growth low, and life span is short.

The second stage is known as the industrial revolution. According to Thompson, as a nation urbanizes it will increase medical and hygienic practices resulting in an increased life expectancy and lowering infant mortality. Combined, these two aspects result in rapid population growth.

In the third stage, or post-industrial revolution stage, of the demographic transition model mature industrial societies begin to emerge. Increased awareness of contraceptive methods, increased education for women, medical practices, and other advancements lead to lowering birth rates. As a result the population size begins to stabilize.

The fourth stage of the demographic transition model characterizes developed countries. This is known as the stabilization stage. At this point, both the birth rates and the death rates are at low levels, resulting in relatively stable population. As with the first stage, population size is steady. Due to increased technology and quality of life, however, the population size will have increased drastically.

Money

The richest 20% of people in the whole world control 80% of the global resources. That means in a small group, two of ten people could control the entire group's money and resources. WOW! The economic growth that happened in the 1980s and 1990s created a bigger gap between the rich and the poor. In the U.S. about 13% of people live below the poverty line. About 40% of those people are children. In the 1990s the largest group of immigrants to the U.S. were Mexicans.

In 2007, the U.S. Census shows that 12.5% of the general population lived in poverty. With 18% of people under age 18 living in poverty this age group has the highest number of people in poverty. According to the census 10.9% of people age 19-64 are in poverty, and only 9.7% of people older than 65 are. In the post World War II period there was a peak in the birth rate which has become known as the baby boom. After this time, the birth rate began to decrease. Years later, the so called baby boomers are reaching old age, making the 65 plus age group the fastest growing group in the United States. This fact is also supported by advances in medical technology which have increased life expectancy.

Thomas Malthus

Thomas Malthus was an influential scholar who was born at the end of the seventeenth century. He theorized that because the world's resources increase at a consistent, or linear rate and the world's population grows exponentially (increasingly faster over time) that there will come a point when there will not be enough resources to support the world's growing population. His ideas influenced many important scientific minds, such as Charles Darwin.

Dependency ratios are connected to Malthus' theories because they describe the relation between the people in a population who cannot work, (the dependents) divided by the number of people who can then multiplied by 100 to give a measure relative to every 100 people. Dependents are considered to be people younger than 15 or older than 64, while workers are anyone in between. Often, the more developed a country is, the lower its dependency ratio. Spain, for example, has a dependency ratio of about 45 people per 100 (in other words 45%). On the other hand Uganda has a dependency ratio of about 110 people per 100 (in other words 110%), meaning there are more dependents than there are workers.

Neo-Malthusian theory builds on and reinforces the theories of Thomas Malthus. Malthus famously argued that due to a disparity between the growth of population and food sources, the world would eventually reach a stage in which resources could no longer support population growth and chaos was ensue. Neo-Malthusian theory supports this, but also looks at further resources such as land, oil, energy, minerals, and others as scarce resources that will soon be overcome by the growing world population. Neo-Malthusian theory strongly advocates use of abortion and birth control in order to curb population growth and preserve these resources.

Urban Sprawl

A metropolitan area, or metropolis, is basically a large city. A metropolis includes the main city and any surrounding suburban areas. Generally, a metropolis has at least 50,000 people in the main city with more in the surrounding areas. Paris and New York are both metropolitan areas. Tokyo is considered the largest metropolitan area in the world. When two or more metropolitan areas that are near each other both grow and their boundaries overlap it is called a megalopolis. An example of a megalopolis in the United States is the Chicago-Detroit-Pittsburgh area.

Urban sprawl is when suburbs and large cities grow so much that they become one large rambling city. This leads to a breakdown of zoning, and parks and open spaces are next door to parking lot structures. Industrialization has made it so that it is no longer necessary for children to work to help support the family as a whole.

Suicide

In 1999, for the first time, the Surgeon General issued a Call To Action To Prevent Suicide, defining it as a "public health hazard." In public interviews he noted how in 1998 for every two homicides in the U.S. there were three suicides. Since 1952, the incidence for adolescents and young adults has nearly tripled, and 90% of these cases were due to guns. Each day 86 Americans take their own lives and another 1,500 attempt to do so.

Two years later, President Bush's new Surgeon General, Dr. David Satcher, repeated the alarm and unveiled a national blueprint to challenge "a preventable problem." No one really knows why people commit suicide and perhaps the person least aware is the victim at the moment of the decision. An estimated 2.9% of the adult population attempts suicide. In efforts to explain this 8th-leading cause of death (third for Americans 15-24), scientists have located the cause of self-destructive behavior both within and without the individual. Physiologists, for instance, have found those with low serotonin (5-hydroxyindoleacetic acid) levels to be as much as ten times more likely to be victims than those with higher amounts. Psychologists talk of precipitators in terms of personality disorders, feelings of hopelessness, helplessness, and alienation, and uncontrollable urges to shed an unwanted self.

The very field of sociology was in part founded on the discovery that suicide rates are as much a sociological phenomenon as they are psychological. Around the turn of the century, French sociologist Emile Durkheim found that single people were more likely to be victims than married individuals, Protestants more likely than Catholics, urban residents more likely than rural folks. Feeling that suicide was related to the nature of the bonds between self and society, **Durkheim** argued that either excessive or deficient levels of integration and regulation lead to four "ideal types" of suicide:

- **egoistic:** perhaps the most prevalent form in the United States, it is the result of too little social integration, such as the suicide of a retired elderly widower;

- **altruistic:** the consequence of excessive integration, such as the death of a Japanese kamikaze pilot during World War II or the self-sacrifice of an Indian suttee, where a widow throws herself upon her husband's funeral pyre;

- **anomic:** results from too little regulation or the shattering of one's ties with society, such as with divorce or unemployment;

- **fatalistic:** this form is the result of excessive regulation coupled with high personal needs to control one's environment, as when a highly motivated college student takes his own life upon failing a critical exam.

Across the United States there is a four-fold difference in rates, ranging from Nevada (23.4 suicides per 100,000 population) and Wyoming (22.4) to New Jersey (7.1) and New York (7.6). Among the major predictors: 1992 divorce rates ($r=.70$), the percent of the population having no religious affiliation ($r=.53$), 1993 fatal accident rates ($.49$), and the percent of the state comprised of Catholics ($r=-.36$).

Turning to international rates, consider the following table from *The Statistical Abstract of the United States 1982-83*, where rates are broken down by age and sex:

COUNTRY	MALE RATES (per 100K)				FEMALE RATES (per 100K)				TOTAL
	15-24	25-44	45-64	65+	15-24	25-44	45-64	65+	
Austria	28.8	40.0	58.1	77.2	6.7	12.7	21.8	31.1	35.5
Switzerland	31.0	39.2	50.6	59.4	13.2	16.3	24.3	22.2	32.5
Denmark	16.3	51.4	71.2	67.7	7.7	25.5	41.1	32.4	29.9
W.Germany	19.0	30.1	40.8	60.4	5.6	12.1	22.0	26.6	27.8
Sweden	16.9	35.3	39.4	42.7	5.8	13.6	19.6	13.2	27.7
France	14.0	25.5	36.2	62.3	5.2	9.1	14.9	21.3	22.9
Japan	16.6	26.8	32.9	51.3	8.2	11.9	16.3	44.4	21.4
Poland	19.5	31.8	34.9	24.7	4.3	4.6	6.3	5.8	19.3
USA	20.0	24.0	25.3	38.0	4.7	8.9	10.5	7.4	18.9
Canada	27.8	30.3	30.2	28.6	5.7	10.1	12.8	8.7	17.2
Australia	17.6	23.1	23.1	25.3	4.5	8.1	8.6	7.9	15.2
Norway	20.4	19.2	30.3	25.0	3.3	8.0	13.0	7.5	14.2
Netherlands	6.2	13.4	20.7	27.8	2.7	9.8	17.7	18.0	10.8
Israel	10.8	9.4	12.9	23.4	1.2	4.3	6.6	15.9	9.6
UK	6.4	14.1	16.6	19.3	3.0	6.0	11.4	12.3	9.1
Ireland	6.2	11.1	12.1	4.3	2.5	4.8	8.4	3.6	6.6

In this sample of basically European countries, observe in the right-most column that there is a five-fold difference in suicide rates between Austria and Ireland. For all age categories, male rates exceed female rates. In eleven of our sixteen countries male rates are highest in old age, while such is the case for females in only seven.

Any analyses of such data must be taken with extreme caution. Undoubtedly there are national differences in the reporting and classification of deaths as suicide and these differences, in turn, probably vary by the sex and age of the deceased. In the United States, for example, suicides of older individuals are more frequently recorded as being due to "natural causes" than is the case for other age groups. With this qualification in mind, let's see what stories might be revealed in this data. First, let us divide female rates by males for each age category. Observe, for instance, that young Austrian women commit suicide at a rate that is 23% that of young Austrian males and that this ratio nearly doubles among Austrians 65 years of age and older:

NATIONAL RATIOS BY AGE OF FEMALE/MALE SUICIDE RATES

COUNTRY	15-24	25-44	45-64	65+
Austria	.23	.32	.38	.40
Switzerland	.43	.42	.48	.37
Denmark	.47	.36	.58	.48
W. Germany	.29	.40	.54	.44
Sweden	.34	.39	.50	.31
France	.37	.36	.41	.34
Japan	.49	.44	.50	.87
Poland	.22	.14	.18	.23
USA	.23	.37	.42	.19
Canada	.21	.33	.42	.30
Australia	.26	.35	.37	.31
Norway	.16	.42	.43	.30
Netherlands	.43	.73	.86	.65
Israel	.11	.46	.51	.68
UK	.47	.43	.69	.64
Ireland	.40	.43	.69	.84

So what inferences are you willing to make about gender differences in the challenges of the life course? In Israel, that Durkheimian bond between self and society certainly appears to be more challenging for young males than for young females, where the ratio of female to male suicide rates is but one-quarter that of Japan and Denmark. And, relative to females, old age appears to be considerably more satisfying to elderly Japanese and Irish males than it is in the United States.

Another way to consider the relative challenges of the life course is to standardize the rates for male and female suicides for those 15-24, 25-44, and 45-64 in terms of their suicide rates in old age. In the table below we find, for instance, that the suicide rate of young Austrian males is 37% that of elderly Austrian males while the suicide rate of young Austrian females is but 22% that of elderly Austrian females:

RATIO OF SUICIDE RATES FOR AGE CATEGORY DIVIDED BY RATE FOR THOSE 65 AND OLDER FOR MEN AND WOMEN BY COUNTRY

COUNTRY	MALE STD. RATES			FEMALE STD. RATES		
	15-24	25-44	45-64	15-24	25-44	45-64
Austria	.37	.52	.75	.22	.41	.70
Switzerland	.52	.66	.85	.59	.73	1.09
Denmark	.24	.76	1.05	.24	.79	1.27
W.Germany	.31	.50	.68	.21	.45	.83
Sweden	.40	.83	.92	.44	1.03	1.48
France	.22	.41	.58	.24	.43	.70
Japan	.32	.52	.64	.18	.27	.37
Poland	.79	1.29	1.41	.74	.79	1.09
USA	.53	.63	.67	.64	1.20	1.42
Canada	.97	1.06	1.06	.66	1.16	1.47
Australia	.70	.91	.91	.57	1.03	1.09
Norway	.82	.77	1.21	.44	1.07	1.73
Netherlands	.22	.48	.74	.15	.54	.98
Israel	.46	.40	.55	.07	.27	.42
UK	.33	.73	.86	.24	.48	.93
Ireland	1.44	2.58	2.81	.69	1.33	2.33

In what countries would you find the challenges of midlife to be considerably greater than those of early adulthood and old age--if you are a male? a female?

According to the U.S. Department of Health and Human Services ("Suicide Among Older Persons, United States, 1980-92, MMWR [Jan. 12, 1996]), age-specific rates of Americans suicides have consistently been highest among older persons. Though accounting for 13% of the populations, older Americans commit nearly one-fifth of all suicides. Though the overall suicide rate for persons 65 and older had been declining from the 1940s through the 1980s, it increased in the late 1980s before once again declining throughout the 1990s. Why the suicide rate of elderly black Americans is but a fraction of that of their white counterparts has intrigued workers. According to a 2002 study by Joan Cook and her colleagues (in the August special suicide issue of The American Journal of Geriatric Psychiatry), the answer may lie in the strong religious faith and social support of African Americans.

Concurrently, the rate of suicide among young adolescents increased 120% from 1980 to 1992. Once extremely rare among teenagers, suicide has become the third-ranking cause of their deaths, after accidents and homicides.

In the United States, in the wake of stories of the right-to-die, Jack Kevorkian, and suicide pacts of elderly couples, the morality of the terminally ill to take their own lives has become a matter of considerable discourse. Since 1977, the National Opinion Research Center has included the following question in its General Social Surveys: "Do you think a person has the right to end his or her own life if this person has an incurable disease?" In 1994, 61% of American adults agreed with this statement compared to 38% seventeen years earlier.

- Support for right of terminally ill to take own lives by age and year. Observe how support consistently declines with age and how, over time, support increases among all age groups.

- Support for right of terminally ill to take own lives by birth cohort and year. Observe how support consistently declines the older the cohort and how, over time, support increases.

- Support for right of terminally ill to take own lives by age, race and sex.

This chart is worth considering in light of the actual suicide rates of these groups:

AGE-ADJUSTED SUICIDE RATES (PER 100,000)
BY RACE AND SEX IN 1991

	MALE	FEMALE
WHITES	19.9	4.8
BLACKS	12.5	1.9

Source: U.S. Department of Health and Human Services. 1993.
Monthly Vital Statistics, vol. 42(2), Tables 10-11 (Aug. 31):38-41.

So what is the bottom line in understanding why people take their own lives? The 1996 suicide (due to overdose of sedatives) of Margaux Hemingway brought back the memories of her grandfather, who committed suicide, as did his brother, sister and father. Is the answer genetic? Do, for instance, people inherit a proclivity toward profound depression which, in turn, predisposes them to be more likely to commit suicide? Or does the Hemingway family story rather indicate an intergenerational socialization pattern where committing suicide when depressed is an acceptable "family way" of addressing the problem? Is the answer purely psychological? Let's say for sake of argument that certain personality types are significantly more predisposed. However, historical and anthropological studies show how different cultures seem to produce distinctive spectrums of personality types and that modal types can change over time. In other words, the proportion of suicide-prone persons in a population is socio-culturally determined. Further, changing social conditions can either trigger or suppress the suicidal urge of these types of selves:

- In Norway, the suicide rate is approximately one-third that of Denmark and Sweden even though all three countries are very similar ethnically, culturally, and geographically. In *Suicide in Different Cultures*, Faberow argues the lower Norwegian rate is due to its more supportive family environments and childrearing practices.

- Studies in the early 1980s, for instance, found that the number of suicides in the U.S. increased by 360 a year for each one percent rise in unemployment.

- Suicides, as well as homicides, plummeted in the country during World War II.

- Being homosexual in a homophobic community can be lethal. A 1989 study for the Department of Health and Human Services estimated that 30 percent of youth suicides are committed by gay and lesbian young people.

- A 1986 study by David P. Phillips and Lundie Carstensen found that between 1973 and 1979 teen-age suicides increased by about 7 percent in the seven days following 38 nationally-televised stories of suicide.

Bottom line: suicide is a highly complex phenomenon that involves the interactions between genetic, biochemical, psychological, societal, and cultural factors.

Emile Durkheim

Emile Durkheim is considered by some to be the father of sociology. Durkheim was born in the mid nineteenth century, and though the popular thought at the time was that individual psychology affected the development or state of society, Durkheim instead believed that society had great impact on individuals. One way he attempted to prove this was through studying suicide. He believed that suicide was a result of social pressures, not individual ones. He was the first to use the term anomie.

Anomie is when a person feels that they lack norms or values or purpose. He believed it to be a cause of suicide. Durkheim believed that when a society had a breakdown of common values or meanings it caused anomic suicide. He is also credited for his theory of functionalism. This theory views society as a type of organism. Every element of society has a function, the main purpose being to maintain balance. These elements include values, traditions, folkways, mores, and other elements used to create normality and stability in a society.

Relative Poverty vs. Absolute Poverty

Simply defined, poverty refers to a state of being extremely poor, or unable to purchase the necessities of life. However, because of social and economic differences throughout the world, poverty can look different for different people. Poverty can be defined in two major categories: absolute poverty and relative poverty.

Absolute poverty occurs when an individual does not have sufficient resources to obtain the minimum essentials of life. For example, if a person cannot obtain shelter, food, and water then they are considered to be in a state of absolute poverty. The qualifications for absolute poverty are generally calculated as a dollar amount of income, although it varies throughout the world based on the cost of living in different areas.

Relative poverty, on the other hand, occurs when individuals are poorer than those around them. This may include a family that lives in a wealthy neighborhood, but lives in a run-down house and has trouble affording the nice things that those around them have. Another example of relative poverty is if an individual loses their job and can no longer afford to maintain their standard of living. Both forms of poverty are damaging to society and individuals.

 # *Dysfunction Types*

In sociology a dysfunction is an event, group, or social entity that has a negative impact on society. Dysfunctions can be either manifest or latent. Manifest dysfunctions are events or elements of society which have a foreseeable negative consequence. For example, a manifest dysfunction of a parade is that it will stop traffic and make it difficult for people to get in and out of the city. On the other hand, latent dysfunctions are unintended negative consequences of an event. For example, schools have the intended positive purpose of education. However, they can also become institutions where gangs can form. The gangs would be considered a latent dysfunction of the school system because it is an unintended negative side effect of it.

 # *Jobs*

For a job to be seen as a profession by a sociologist, it must be something that can only be done with a conceptual knowledge and specialized information and training.

Sample Test Questions

1) Malthus predicted that the population will grow at an exponential rate and rapidly exceed its ability to sustain itself. The solution he proposed for this problem is

   A) Moral restraint
   B) Three child policy
   C) Sex education
   D) Contraception
   E) Abortion

The correct answer is: A:) Moral restraint. Malthus argued that there were preventive checks of moral restraints such as abstinence, delaying of marriage until financially stable, and restricting marriage with people who suffer from poverty.

2) Absolute poverty refers to a state wherein an individual are deprived of the resources which are essential for subsistence of poverty line while relative poverty refers to

   A) Individuals who lacks resources in cultural aspects
   B) Individuals who are in demand for more resources
   C) Individuals who are unemployed
   D) Individuals who are unexperienced in the working force
   E) Individuals who lack resources when compared to other members of the society

The correct answer is: E:) Individuals who lack resources when compared to other members of the society. The concept of relative poverty is used to measure the degree of a person's poverty. Accordingly, people become poor because they are deprived of opportunities, comfort and self-respect which are regarded as normal in the community where they belong.

3) The meaning of dependency ratio is

 A) Portion of population composed of people who are productive in the labor force
 B) Portion of population composed of people who are too young or old to work
 C) Portion of population composed of people who are unemployed
 D) Portion of population composed of people who are businessmen
 E) Portion of population composed of people who are working internationally

The correct answer is: B:) Portion of population composed of people who are too young or old to work. The dependency ratio is a measurement to show the number of dependents in a population. The age ranges from zero to 14 and over the age of 65, to the total population, aged 15 to 64.

4) Which among below does not make up demographics?

 A) Mortality
 B) Age structure
 C) Population growth
 D) Scientific explanations
 E) Fertility

The correct answer is: D:) Scientific explanations. Demographics is the statistical study of populations of human beings. In general science, it analyzes any kind of dynamic living population. Demography comprehends the study of the size, structure, and distribution of these populations.

5) The correct equation for population growth is

 A) (Births - Deaths) + (Immigrants + Emigrants) = Growth
 B) (Births + Deaths) + (Immigrants - Emigrants) = Growth
 C) (Births - Deaths) + (Emigrants - Immigrants) = Growth
 D) (Births - Deaths) + (Immigrants - Emigrants) = Growth
 E) (Deaths - Births) + (Immigrants - Emigrants) = Growth

The correct answer is: D:) (Births - Deaths) + (Immigrants - Emigrants) = Growth. The components of a population change is composed of the addition of Natural Increase and Net Migration to get the result of Population Growth.

6) What is a less intimate group where people pursue the same goals without a sense of belonging?

   A) Aggregate
   B) Primary group
   C) Secondary group
   D) Census
   E) Sample

The correct answer is C:) Secondary group.

7) Set of manners that are a part of everyday life in society

   A) Values
   B) Norms
   C) Deviance
   D) Folkways
   E) Ascribed status

The correct answer is D:) Folkways.

8) A position given to those who have not achieved things on their own

   A) Values
   B) Norms
   C) Deviance
   D) Folkways
   E) Ascribed status

The correct answer is E:) Ascribed status.

9) Which of the following best describes the power elite?

   A) The middle level of power which deals with relatively minor issues.
   B) The lowest level of power which consists of the masses with no decision making power.
   C) The largest group of people who work together to make important decisions.
   D) A small group of people who regularly make important decisions for the country.
   E) The multiple groups of people in the government with power and decision making abilities.

The correct answer is D:) A small group of people who regularly make important decisions for the country. The power elite are the smallest group of people who make the most important decisions.

10) A set of cases randomly chosen from a large group?

    A) Aggregate
    B) Primary group
    C) Secondary group
    D) Census
    E) Sample

The correct answer is E:) Sample.

11) Similar in structure of organization

    A) Qualitative
    B) Social solidarity
    C) Social conflict
    D) Populations
    E) Quantitative

The correct answer is A:) Qualitative.

12) A person takes a bowling class at their local community college. They enjoy interacting with the other members in the class on a weekly basis. Is the class a primary or secondary group? Choose the MOST correct answer.

    A) It is a primary group because they interact face to face and likely will become close friends.
    B) It is a primary group because they share common interests and care for each other's wellbeing.
    C) It is a secondary group because they see each other regularly and share a common interest.
    D) It is a secondary group because they share only one common interest and are not emotionally close.
    E) None of the above

The correct answer is D:) It is a secondary group because they share only one common interest and are not emotionally close. This is the best answer because even though the members share a common interest, they see each other only once a week and likely are not emotionally close. Although it may develop into a primary group, the class is secondary.

13) Something measurable

    A) Qualitative
    B) Social solidarity
    C) Social conflict
    D) Populations
    E) Quantitative

The correct answer is E:) Quantitative.

14) People who share the same geographic area

    A) Qualitative
    B) Social solidarity
    C) Social conflict
    D) Population
    E) Quantitative

The correct answer is D:) Population.

15) Ideals about what is desirable in behavior

    A) Values
    B) Norms
    C) Deviance
    D) Folkways
    E) Ascribed status

The correct answer is A:) Values.

16) Which age group is the fastest growing the United States?

    A) Under 18 years
    B) 18-30 years
    C) 31-45 years
    D) 46-64 years
    E) 65+ years

The correct answer is E:) 65+ years. This is a result of both the so called baby boom and advances in medical technology.

17) Rules the define expected behavior

    A) Values
    B) Norms
    C) Deviance
    D) Folkways
    E) Ascribed status

The correct answer is B:) Norms.

18) The term false consciousness is derived from the theories of

    A) Emile Durkheim
    B) Karl Marx
    C) Christine Williams
    D) Max Weber
    E) William J Goode

The correct answer is B:) Karl Marx.

19) Anything that is perceived by society as outside the norm

    A) Values
    B) Norms
    C) Deviance
    D) Folkways
    E) Ascribed status

The correct answer is C:) Deviance.

20) A statistician is gathering data to prove a hypothesis. He begins by using a survey, which shows that he is incorrect. However, he is not convinced and moves on to using an experiment to test his hypothesis. He is still proven incorrect. Frustrated, the statistician asks a friend to test the hypothesis as well, and they also prove it incorrect. The statistician must conclude that his hypothesis is in fact incorrect. He has used the research method of

   A) Dramaturgy
   B) Gesellschaft
   C) Triangulation
   D) Amonie
   E) None of the above

The correct answer is C:) Triangulation. This is when a claim is cross referenced using three or more methods or sources, as the statistician did.

21) Customs that are important to culture

   A) Mores
   B) Law
   C) Culture
   D) Role
   E) Anomie

The correct answer is A:) Mores.

22) Demographics is integral to the study of

   A) Mathematics
   B) Sociology
   C) Psychology
   D) Linguistics
   E) None of the above

The correct answer B:) Sociology. Demographics is the study of populations, and sociology is the study of societies, so the two have a lot of overlap.

23) A family moves to the United States from Korea. The family speaks both Korean and English with each other. While they celebrate many national holidays of the United States, they also celebrate holidays from Korea and enjoy sharing the Korean culture with their neighbors. They have

    A) Integrated
    B) Amalgamated
    C) Assimilated
    D) Corrupted
    E) None of the above

The correct answer is A:) Integrated. The family has combined their old culture with their new culture.

24) A person walking to school is accidentally tripped by a stranger, the stranger hurries to apologize and the person assures them it is fine. Later, the same person is accidentally tripped by a younger sibling, who also apologizes, however this time the person becomes angry. The effect of situation on the person's response is called

    A) Dramaturgy
    B) Amalgamation
    C) Situational discrimination
    D) Anomie
    E) Fecundity

The correct answer is A:) Dramaturgy.

25) Which religion believes that Jesus Christ was the son of God?

    A) Christianity
    B) Judaism
    C) Islam
    D) Hinduism
    E) Buddhism

The correct answer is A:) Christianity.

26) Who wrote *Gender Differences at Work: Women and Men in Nontraditional Occupations*?

   A) George Mead
   B) William J Goode
   C) Christine Williams
   D) Charles Wright Mills
   E) Emile Durkheim

The correct answer is C:) Christine Williams.

27) The existence of multiple cultural groups in the same area is

   A) Dramaturgy
   B) Oligopoly
   C) Cultural pluralism
   D) Gameinschaft
   E) Halo effect

The correct answer is C:) Cultural pluralism.

28) Creation of standards

   A) Cultural relativism
   B) Ethnocentrism
   C) Accommodation
   D) Assimilation
   E) Normative order

The correct answer is E:) Normative order.

29) A society which is matrilineal will often also be

   A) Matrilocal
   B) Patrilocal
   C) Patrilineal
   D) Neolocal
   E) Egalitarian

The correct answer is A:) Matrilocal.

30) Which religion believes in reincarnation?

    A) Christianity
    B) Judaism
    C) Islam
    D) Hinduism
    E) Buddhism

The correct answer is D:) Hinduism.

31) Durkheim developed a theory of functionalism, in which elements of society are used to maintain balance. According to Durkheim, these elements include

    A) Roads and other infrastructure
    B) Commerce and trade
    C) Traditions, folkways and mores
    D) Both A and C
    E) All of the above

The correct answer is C:) Traditions, folkways and mores. Durkheim believed that these, and other elements, were used to create normality and stability in a society.

32) Set of expectations of a person's behavior based on their position in society

    A) Mores
    B) Law
    C) Culture
    D) Role
    E) Anomie

The correct answer is D:) Role.

33) A society in which a husband is expected to move in with his wife's family is

    A) Neolocal
    B) Matrilineal
    C) Patrilocal
    D) Matrilocal
    E) Nuclear

The correct answer is D:) Matrilocal.

34) Who researched and created the idea of groupthink?

    A) Karl Marx
    B) Emile Durkheim
    C) Georg Simmel
    D) C. Wright Mills
    E) Irving Janis

The correct answer is E:) Irving Janis.

35) Which of the following correctly identifies the ratio of women to men in the 85+ age group?

    A) Nearly one fourth
    B) Nearly half
    C) Exactly even
    D) Nearly double
    E) More than four times as many

The correct answer is D:) Nearly double. In the 85+ group there are twice as many women as men.

36) The Amish people in Pennsylvania have their own distinct customs, use their own banks, stores, schools and use no electricity. However, their customs are generally accepted by people in the surrounding areas. This is called

    A) Cultural pluralism
    B) Halo effect
    C) Glass ceiling
    D) Endogamy
    E) None of the above

The correct answer is A:) Cultural pluralism.

37) Who studied group interactions?

    A) Karl Marx
    B) Emile Durkheim
    C) Georg Simmel
    D) C. Wright Mills
    E) Irving Janis

The correct answer is D:) C. Wright Mills.

38) A person who is of a certain religion refuses to marry anyone who is not of their same religion. This is an example of

    A) Endogamy
    B) Dramaturgy
    C) Halo effect
    D) Exogamy
    E) Gameinschaft

The correct answer is A:) Endogamy. The person is marrying within their own cultural group.

39) Instability in a culture because of the erosion of morals

    A) Mores
    B) Law
    C) Culture
    D) Role
    E) Anomie

The correct answer is E:) Anomie.

40) What is the minimum amount of people for a metropolis?

    A) 500
    B) 5,000
    C) 50,000
    D) 500,000
    E) 5,000,000

The correct answer is C:) 50,000. This includes the people in the main city. There are generally more in the surrounding areas as well.

41) In which system the resources are privately owned?

    A) Capitalism
    B) Socialism
    C) Communism
    D) Fatalism
    E) None of the above

The correct answer is A:) Capitalism.

42) A family in which the father is the dominant parent is

    A) Patrilineal
    B) Patriarchal
    C) Patrilocal
    D) Patridomant
    E) Egalitarian

The correct answer is B:) Patriarchal. Patrilineal is when the father's lineage is more important than the mother's, and patrilocal is when the wife is expected to move in with her husband's family. Egalitarian is when the parents share dominance.

43) Which of the following is NOT an institution?

    A) Government
    B) Family
    C) Medicine
    D) Religion
    E) Peer group

The correct answer is E:) Peer group.

44) In a monopoly a product is

    A) Sold by only one company and there is no close substitute available.
    B) Sold by only a few companies, who have great influence over the market.
    C) Sold by hundreds of companies in competition with each other.
    D) Sold by one company, though there are many close substitutes available.
    E) None of the above

The correct answer is A:) Sold by only one company and there is no close substitute available.

45) Which of the following was NOT one of Weber's characteristics for an effective bureaucracy?

    A) Division of labor
    B) Implied rule systems
    C) Impersonality
    D) Clear goals and purposes
    E) Specialized labor

The correct answer is B:) Implied rule systems. Weber believed that there needed to be specific and clearly defined formal systems of rules.

46) When the meaning of a trait depends on a cultural background it is called

    A) Cultural relativism
    B) Ethnocentrism
    C) Accommodation
    D) Assimilation
    E) Normative order

The correct answer is A:) Cultural relativism.

47) What did William J Goode believe had an affect on divorce rates?

    A) Industrialization
    B) Geography
    C) Population size
    D) Number of children in a family
    E) None of the above

The correct answer is A:) Industrialization. This is one theory which he discussed in his book *World Revolution and Family Patterns*.

48) When a person things that everyone should be just like themselves

    A) Cultural relativism
    B) Ethnocentrism
    C) Accommodation
    D) Assimilation
    E) Normative order

The correct answer is B:) Ethnocentrism.

49) Which of the following is NOT an example of vertical mobility?

    A) McDonald's employee to lawyer
    B) Industrial worker to doctor
    C) Janitor to Governor
    D) Construction worker to surgeon
    E) All of the above are examples of vertical mobility

The correct answer is E:) All of the above are examples of vertical mobility. All of the answers involve a status change.

50) The difference made to your mind by the proves of assimilation

    A) Cultural relativism
    B) Ethnocentrism
    C) Accommodation
    D) Assonance
    E) Normative order

The correct answer is C:) Accommodation.

51) Which of the following BEST describes the resource mobilization theory?

    A) If people do not have a plan for resource mobilization, during times of war there will be no way for the government or people to access resources necessary for life.
    B) Social movements are organizations which use resources to achieve rational goals.
    C) If the current pattern continues, there will come a point when humankind's need for resources outstrips the world's ability to produce resources.
    D) As the lower class feels more and more oppressed, it eventually rises up against higher class and overthrows the social system, instead instituting a classless society.
    E) None of the above

The correct answer is B:) Social movements are organizations which use resources to achieve rational goals.

52) Rules created by the government

    A) Mores
    B) Law
    C) Culture
    D) Role
    E) Anomie

The correct answer is B:) Law.

53) A society in which a wife is expected to move in with her husband's family is

    A) Neolocal
    B) Nuclear
    C) Matrilineal
    D) Patrilineal
    E) Patrilocal

The correct answer is E:) Patrilocal.

54) Beliefs, norms, values and attitudes

    A) Mores
    B) Law
    C) Culture
    D) Role
    E) Anomie

The correct answer is C:) Culture.

55) According to Marx, poverty was a direct result of what?

    A) Laziness
    B) Capitalism
    C) Socialism
    D) Exploitation of the proletariat by the bourgeoisie
    E) Exploitation of the bourgeoisie by the proletariat

The correct answer is B:) Capitalism. According to Marx, the exploitation of the proletariat by the bourgeoisie was a result of capitalism.

56) The process by which a person takes material into their mind from the environment

    A) Cultural relativism
    B) Ethnocentrism
    C) Accommodation
    D) Assimilation
    E) Normative order

The correct answer is D:) Assimilation.

57) A mother, child, grandmother and aunt make up a

    A) Nuclear family
    B) Blended family
    C) Extended family
    D) Kibbutz
    E) None of the above

The correct answer is C:) Extended family.

58) A student wishes to know what the most popular type of music is in their school. What type of variable are they interested in?

    A) Numerical
    B) Quantitative
    C) Qualitative
    D) Significant
    E) None of the above

The correct answer is C:) Qualitative. Qualitative variables are also referred to as categorical. They are variables which are not dealt with in numerical terms, like styles of music.

59) Which case outlawed segregation in schools?

    A) Marbury vs. Madison
    B) Plessy vs. Ferguson
    C) McCulloch vs. Maryland
    D) Brown vs. Board of Education
    E) Dred Scott vs. Sandford

The correct answer is D:) Brown vs. Board of Education.

    www.PassYourClass.com

60) What is the halo effect?

 A) The law which governs the relation between supply and demand and the cost of products.
 B) The theory which describes how people's perception of one trait is affected by their knowledge about another trait.
 C) A theoretical barrier preventing women and minorities from advancing due to discrimination.
 D) A tangible barrier which prevents people from entering important governmental buildings without identification.
 E) None of the above

The correct answer is B:) The theory which describes how people's perception of one trait is affected by their knowledge about another trait.

61) Which system was portrayed in Animal Farm?

 A) Capitalism
 B) Socialism
 C) Communism
 D) Fatalism
 E) None of the above

The correct answer is B:) Socialism.

62) In which system does the government have rigid control of their citizens and their lives?

 A) Monarchy
 B) Totalitarianism
 C) Communism
 D) Dictatorship
 E) Democracy

The correct answer is B:) Totalitarianism.

63) Which of the following is the BEST example of an oligopoly?

    A) Potato farming
    B) Gas stations
    C) Restaurants
    D) Clothing
    E) None of the above

The correct answer is B:) Gas stations. As with cell phones, there are few small gas station companies. Most companies are large and they have great influence over each other's policies and prices.

64) A step-mother, child and father makes up a

    A) Nuclear family
    B) Blended family
    C) Extended family
    D) Kibbutz
    E) None of the above

The correct answer is B:) Blended family.

65) When one woman marries more than one man

    A) Endogamy
    B) Exogamy
    C) Monogamy
    D) Polygamy
    E) Polyandry

The correct answer is E:) Polyandry.

66) Which of the following correctly states the dependency ratio?

    A) Dependents / workers
    B) Workers x dependents
    C) Dependents - workers
    D) Workers / dependents
    E) Workers - dependents

The correct answer is A:) Dependents / workers.

67) An individual moves to the United States from Egypt. They feel out of place and begin to do everything they can to fit in better. They change their style and stop speaking Arabic. Eventually most people come to assume they were actually born in the United States. They have

    A) Integrated
    B) Amalgamated
    C) Assimilated
    D) Corrupted
    E) None of the above

The correct answer is C:) Assimilated. They have adapted to fit into the society, leaving their old culture behind.

68) A mother, father, daughter and son make up a

    A) Nuclear family
    B) Blended family
    C) Extended family
    D) Kibbutz
    E) None of the above

The correct answer is A:) Nuclear family.

69) Which of the following is NOT a type of mobility?

    A) Anomic
    B) Intergenerational
    C) Intragenerational
    D) Horizontal
    E) Vertical

The correct answer is A:) Anomic. Intergenerational, intragenerational, horizontal, and vertical are all types of social mobility.

70) When members of different classes or groups marry

    A) Endogamy
    B) Exogamy
    C) Monogamy
    D) Polygamy
    E) Polyandry

The correct answer is B:) Exogamy.

71) Who introduced the idea of gameinschaft and gesellschaft?

    A) Emile Durkheim
    B) George Mead
    C) Ferdinand Tonnies
    D) Christine Williams
    E) Max Weber

The correct answer is C:) Ferdinand Tonnies.

72) Which of the following is an example of an amalgamation?

    A) Canadians
    B) Mestizos
    C) Chileans
    D) Scandinavians
    E) All of the above

The correct answer is B:) Mestizos. Mestizo is the term for people of mixed Native American and European descent.

73) Which of the following is a measure of the reproductive potential of a population?

    A) Dramaturgy
    B) Demographics
    C) Oligopoly
    D) Fecundity
    E) Glass ceiling

The correct answer is D:) Fecundity.

74) When one man and one woman marry

    A) Endogamy
    B) Exogamy
    C) Monogamy
    D) Polygamy
    E) Polyandry

The correct answer is C:) Monogamy.

75) Which of the following is the most common family structure in the United States?

A) Nuclear
B) Matriarchal
C) Extended
D) Non family household
E) None of the above

The correct answer is A:) Nuclear. Just over half of all families in the United States are nuclear.

76) A group of two people is called a

A) Dyad
B) Tryad
C) Group
D) Dynamic
E) None of the above

The correct answer is A:) Dyad.

77) What age group is used in calculating the fecundity of a population?

A) Men age 15 to 44
B) Women age 15 to 44
C) Men older than 44
D) Women older than 44
E) Both A and B

The correct answer is B:) Women 15 to 44. The fecundity is the reproductive potential of a population, and is measured using women between the ages of 15 and 44.

78) According to Marx's conflict theory, what is the privileged class with control of resources who are overthrown by the exploited class?

A) Power elite
B) Proletariat
C) Aristocracy
D) Bourgeoisie
E) None of the above

The correct answer is D:) Bourgeoisie.

79) Which of the following, when broken, will yield the worst punishment?

    A) Norms
    B) Folkways
    C) Anomies
    D) Mores
    E) All are equal

The correct answer is D:) Mores. A person who breaks a folkway will face mild reactions, whereas a person who violates mores will face disgust and punishment.

80) Which of the following is closest to amalgamation?

    A) Monopolization
    B) Division
    C) Merging
    D) Replacement
    E) Distribution

The correct answer is C:) Merging. Amalgamation refers to a mixing of two previously separate groups.

81) When one man marries more than one woman

    A) Endogamy
    B) Exogamy
    C) Monogamy
    D) Polygamy
    E) Polyandry

The correct answer is D:) Polygamy.

82) When a person feels that they lack values of purpose it is called

    A) Anomie
    B) Glass Ceiling
    C) Gameinschaft
    D) Dramaturgy
    E) Gesellschaft

The correct answer is A:) Anomie.

83) False consciousness stops people from seeing their potential for

    A) Horizontal mobility
    B) Self actualization
    C) Upward mobility
    D) Dramaturgy
    E) Exogamy

The correct answer is C:) Upward mobility. This comes from a misrepresentation in which the higher classes purposely attempt to make lower classes view themselves as subordinate.

84) Who wrote *The Power Elite*?

    A) George Mead
    B) William J Goode
    C) Christine Williams
    D) C. Wright Mills
    E) Emile Durkheim

The correct answer is D:) C. Wright Mills.

85) Which of the following best describes the glass ceiling?

    A) The law which governs the relation between supply and demand and the cost of products.
    B) The theory which describes how people's perception of one trait is affected by their knowledge about another trait.
    C) A theoretical barrier preventing women and minorities from advancing due to discrimination.
    D) A tangible barrier which prevents people from entering important governmental buildings without identification.
    E) None of the above

The correct answer is C:) A theoretical barrier preventing women and minorities from advancing due to discrimination.

86) Which of the following studied suicide?

A) Karl Marx
B) Emile Durkheim
C) Georg Simmel
D) C. Wright Mills
E) Irving Janis

The correct answer is B:) Emile Durkheim.

87) Which of the following is the BEST example of an ethnic group?

A) Ethiopians
B) Quakers
C) African Americans
D) Caucasians
E) Belgians

The correct answer is B:) Quakers. Quakers are a religious group, whereas all the other options describe either a nationality or a race.

88) In triangulation, how many methods must claims be validated through?

A) Five
B) Two
C) One
D) Three or more
E) None of the above

The correct answer is D:) Three or more.

89) George Mead developed which of the following theories?

A) Social interactionist theory
B) Conflict theory
C) Attachment theory
D) Characteristics of efficient bureaucracy
E) The existence of power elite

The correct answer is A:) Social interactionist theory.

90) Who coined the term "power elite"?

   A) Karl Marx
   B) Emile Durkheim
   C) Georg Simmel
   D) C. Wright Mills
   E) Irving Janis

The correct answer is D:) C. Wright Mills.

91) Societies in which the lineage of the husband and wife are equally important are

   A) Neolineal
   B) Neolocal
   C) Egalitarian
   D) Bilineal
   E) Patrilineal

The correct answer is D:) Bilineal.

92) When someone follows the group it is called

   A) Passiveness
   B) Groupthink
   C) Anomie
   D) Group
   E) Aggregate

The correct answer is B:) Groupthink.

93) Which of the following words most correctly describes how ethnic groups are classified?

   A) Culture
   B) Ancestry
   C) Citizenship
   D) Religion
   E) Physical traits

The correct answer is A:) Culture. Although religions are a type of ethnic group, culture is a more correct answer because it includes religion along with other aspects which determine ethnicity.

94) Which of the following is NOT an element of culture?

  A) Custom
  B) Language
  C) Values or beliefs
  D) Population
  E) All of the above

The correct answer is D:) Population. Population is an element of demographics.

95) A person is arrested for burglary and the prosecutor allows them to plead guilty to attempted burglary. This is called a(n)

  A) Appeal
  B) Charge bargain
  C) Habeas corpus
  D) Malfeasance
  E) Sentence bargain

The correct answer is B:) Charge bargain. They pled guilty to a different charge with less severe consequences.

96) When we think a celebrity must be good with children and money because of their status and money it is called

  A) Groupthink
  B) Dramaturgy
  C) Halo effect
  D) Celebrity status
  E) None of the above

The correct answer is C:) Halo effect.

Use this scenario for the next two questions.

A new type of pain medication for arthritis patients has just been developed. Before going on the market, it has to be run through clinical trials to be tested for safety and effectiveness. Many sufferers applied and 150 people suffering from pain due to arthritis are asked to participate in the trials. The people are split into two groups of 75. The first group is given one pill a day, and the second is given two pills a day. The people asked to rate their pain on a scale of one to ten after one week.

97) What is the dependent variable?

    A) Amount of medicine received
    B) Whether or not the person is in the trial
    C) How long the person has been experiencing pain
    D) The amount of pain relief
    E) None of the above

The correct answer is D:) The amount of pain relief. This is the variable which is being measured.

98) What is the independent variable?

    A) Amount of medicine received
    B) Whether or not the person is in the trial
    C) How long the person has been experiencing pain
    D) The amount of pain relief
    E) None of the above

The correct answer is A:) Amount of medicine received. This is the variable which will affect the other, and which is independent of the other.

99) What leaves no visible victim?

    A) Deviance
    B) White collar crime
    C) Working class
    D) Blue collar crime
    E) None of the above

The correct answer is B:) White collar crime.

100) Determine the mean of the following set of numbers

23, 24, 27, 25, 26, 24, 28, 3, 6, 1

    A) 26
    B) 23.5
    C) 24.5
    D) 15.2
    E) 18.7

The correct answer is E:) 18.7. The mean is 18.7 and the median is 23.5.

101) Which of the following is NOT an element of demographics?

    A) Population size
    B) Death rate
    C) Location
    D) Income level
    E) All of the above are elements of demographics

The correct answer is E:) All of the above are elements of demographics. While it may not seem that location is an element of demographics, it is considered to be so because a society's environment can affect its behavior.

102) According to Tonnies, the best example of gameinschaft was a

    A) Corporation
    B) School
    C) Government office
    D) Family
    E) Group of friends

The correct answer is D:) Family. Gameinschaft is a situation in which the condition of the group is more important than the individual, and Tonnies believed this to be like a family.

103) Which of the following are NOT white collar crimes?

    A) Embezzling
    B) Tnsider trading
    C) Tax evasion
    D) Assault
    E) Operating without a license

The correct answer is D:) Assault.

104) A person is raised in a highly industrial city and their family is quite wealthy. However, they marry a person from a poor southern farming town. This is an example of

A) Endogamy
B) Dramaturgy
C) Halo effect
D) Exogamy
E) Gameinschaft

The correct answer is D:) Exogamy. The person is marrying outside their own wealthy and industrialized culture.

105) A social group with intense intimacy

A) Aggregate
B) Primary group
C) Secondary group
D) Census
E) Sample

The correct answer is B:) Primary group.

106) Which of the following is NOT a secondary group?

A) Quilting clubs
B) Sports teams
C) Nuclear family
D) Alcoholics Anonymous
E) Both C and D

The correct answer is C:) Nuclear family. Families interact with each other and care about each other's well being. This makes them primary groups.

107) A collection of data from all cases or people in the chosen set

A) Aggregate
B) Primary group
C) Secondary group
D) Census
E) Sample

The correct answer is D:) Census.

108) Which age group has the highest number of people in poverty?

    A) Under 18 years
    B) 18-30 years
    C) 31-45 years
    D) 46-64 years
    E) 65+ years

The correct answer is A:) Under 18 years.

109) In which system is a queen or king present?

    A) Monarchy
    B) Socialism
    C) Communism
    D) Dictatorship
    E) Democracy

The correct answer is A:) Monarchy.

110) Which of the following best describes the relation between culture and society?

    A) Cultures can be described by their society
    B) Cultures and societies are interchangeable terms
    C) Societies can be described by their cultures
    D) Cultures and Societies will always have opposite characteristics
    E) None of the above

The correct answer is C:) Societies can be described by their cultures. Society is a collection of individuals with similar characteristics, which can include culture.

111) Who wrote the book *World Revolution and Family Patterns*?

    A) George Mead
    B) William J Goode
    C) Christine Williams
    D) Charles Wright Mills
    E) Emile Durkheim

The correct answer is B:) William J Goode.

112) Which of the following is largest?

    A) Village
    B) Town
    C) City
    D) Megalopolis
    E) Metropolis

The correct answer is D:) Megalopolis. A megalopolis is occurs when a metropolis grows and overlaps with another metropolis.

113) The emotional intensity of the attachments in a group

    A) Qualitative
    B) Social solidarity
    C) Social conflict
    D) Populations
    E) Quantitative

The correct answer is B:) Social solidarity.

114) Which age groups are considered dependents?

I. Younger than 15
II. From 15-64
III. Older than 64

    A) I only
    B) III only
    C) I and II only
    D) II and III only
    E) I and III only

The correct answer is E:) I and III only.

115) A person is charged with manslaughter and the prosecutor allows them to plead guilty for a short sentence instead of going to trial. This is called a(n)

A) Appeal
B) Charge bargain
C) Habeas corpus
D) Malfeasance
E) Sentence bargain

The correct answer is E:) Sentence bargain. When the person agrees to plead guilty to receive a shorter sentence it is called a sentence bargain.

116) Determine the mean and median of the following set of numbers respectively

2, 4, 7, 23, 27, 28 , 4, 26

A) 15.1, 18.5
B) 15.1, 23
C) 23, 15.1
D) 18.5, 15.1
E) 16.1, 7

The correct answer is A:) 15.1, 18.5. The median is 18.5 because there is an even amount of numbers. When this happens, the two middle numbers are averaged together. In this case (7+27)/2=18.5

117) Unfriendly interaction between groups

A) Qualitative
B) Social solidarity
C) Social conflict
D) Populations
E) Quantitative

The correct answer is C:) Social conflict.

118) Which of the following sociologists developed a theory of effective characteristics for bureaucracies?

A) Emile Durkheim
B) George Mead
C) William J Goode
D) Christine Williams
E) Max Weber

The correct answer is E:) Max Weber.

119) Who developed the term glass escalator?

A) Christine Williams
B) Warren Thompson
C) Arlie Hochschild
D) George Mead
E) Immanuel Wallerstein

The correct answer is A:) Christine Williams. The term refers to the tendency of males to do better in female-dominated fields than females in male-dominated fields.

120) The pluralist model describes the distribution of power within a society as

A) Centralized to a few high government officials
B) Dispersed fairly and equally throughout the population
C) Fragmented and divided among many small groups
D) Closely held in balance between corporations and government
E) None of the above

The correct answer is C:) Fragmented and divided among many small groups. According to the model, the groups are able to work with government in order to find solutions to problems and advocate for their concerns. Because the power is broadly distributed among several groups negotiation is used and often leads to outcomes and solutions that are fair and well-reasoned.

121) Differential association theory claims that

    A) Socialization is the lifelong process that an individual goes through as they develop their sense of self
    B) Overpopulation is a major concern and must be handled through the use of birth control
    C) Having multiple social roles leads to a conflict of self and difficulty of establishing an identity
    D) Crime is a behavior that is learned by association
    E) Broad distribution of power allows for the best societal outcomes

The correct answer is D:) Crime is a behavior that is learned by association. The theory was developed by criminologist Edwin Sutherland. He believed that through exposure and learning, criminal behaviors become the norm for certain individuals.

122) According to Mead's stages of self, which stage is characterized by simple imitation?

    A) Precognitive
    B) Preparation
    C) Play
    D) Game
    E) Analytical

The correct answer is B:) Preparation. Mead's three stages are preparation, play, and game. Each is characterized by an increased level of understanding and ability to assimilate societal expectations into play. Preparation occurs during the first year or so of life in which a child is capable only of imitating the actions around them.

123) Neo-Malthusian theory advocates

    A) Gender equality
    B) Discrimination
    C) Birth control
    D) Double consciousness
    E) None of the above

The correct answer is C:) Birth control. Neo-Malthusian theory builds on the fears of Thomas Malthus that the world was becoming overpopulated. Neo-Malthusian theory strongly advocates use of abortion and birth control in order to curb population growth and preserve resources.

124) Absolute poverty occurs when

    A) An entire society is relatively poorer than those around them
    B) An entire society is living below normal living standards
    C) An individual has absolutely no income
    D) An individual is poorer than the people around them
    E) An individual cannot obtain the basic necessities of life

The correct answer is E:) An individual cannot obtain the basic necessities of life. Absolute poverty occurs when an individual does not have sufficient resources to obtain the minimum essentials of life. Relative poverty, on the other hand, occurs when individuals are poorer than those around them.

125) Which of the following is an example of manifest dysfunction?

    A) Gangs developing in high schools
    B) Cell phones being used to improve communications
    C) A flyswatter being used to smash flies in a house
    D) Loud noise from a party disrupting neighbors
    E) All of the above

The correct answer is D:) Loud noise from a party disrupting neighbors. Manifest dysfunctions are events or elements of society which have a foreseeable negative consequence. On the other hand, latent dysfunctions are unintended negative consequences of an event.

126) Who wrote the book The Second Shift?

    A) Edwin Sutherland
    B) George Mead
    C) Arlie Russell Hochschild
    D) Immanuel Wallerstein
    E) Warren Thompson

The correct answer is C:) Arlie Russell Hochschild. Arlie Russell Hochschild is known for her book The Second Shift that discusses the role of women in the workplace. Hochschild notes in her book that working mothers essentially have a second shift when they return home from full time jobs.

127) Double consciousness occurs when

    A) A population develops extremes of wealth and poverty with little middle class
    B) An individual experiences a head injury and cannot remember who they are
    C) A group cannot decide between two different courses of action
    D) An individual experiences a feeling of having two competing social identities
    E) None of the above

The correct answer is D:) An individual experiences a feeling of having two competing social identities. The phenomenon was first discussed by W.E.B. DuBois to describe the feeling he experienced as an African American trying to assimilate into the larger U.S. culture.

128) According to the world systems theory, the core regions are those which

    A) Are more developed and hold economic, military and social advantages
    B) Are semi-developed and lack the sophistication of urbanized communities
    C) Are underdeveloped and impoverished
    D) Are centrally located between important world markets
    E) Are militarily powerful but lack sophisticated economies

The correct answer is A:) Are more developed and hold economic, military and social advantages. The theory was developed by Immanuel Wallerstein to described development in the modern world. It divides nations into those that are core, semi-periphery, and periphery. Core regions are the most developed, while periphery are the least.

129) Which of the following is true according to the demographic transition theory?

    A) Improving medical practices will not affect infant mortality
    B) Increasing hygienic practices will not affect the growth of the population
    C) Pre-industrial societies have low infant mortality
    D) Population growth is greatest in the final stage of transition
    E) Stabilized countries have low population growth

The correct answer is E:) Stabilized countries have low population growth. This development theory states four different stages of development. The fourth, Stabilization, results in large population size due to medical technology and education, but low population growth.

130) Which of the following is NOT an example of cultural pluralism?

    A) Chinatown
    B) Amish
    C) Native American reservations
    D) Politicians
    E) All of the above

The correct answer is D:) Politicians. Cultural pluralism occurs when ethnic groups within a society are able to keep their individual cultures while still living within the larger society. In the United States phenomenon such as Chinatown, the Amish people, and Native American reservations are all examples of this.

131) What is the dependency ratio?

    A) Ratio of those in poverty to the total population
    B) Ratio of dependents within a society to the total population
    C) Ratio of people living on welfare to the total population
    D) Ratio of babies born each year to the total population
    E) None of the above

The correct answer is B:) Ratio of dependents within a society to the total population. The dependency ratio is calculated by totaling the number of dependents (those younger than fourteen and older than 65) and dividing by the remaining population (those aged 15-64).

132) Triangulation occurs when

    A) Three individuals all focus their attention on a single other person to make them feel alienated
    B) Three tests are used to determine whether an individual has a particular illness or not
    C) A person uses three sources of advice before making a decision
    D) An individual refuses to confront the person that they are angry with and instead goes to a third party
    E) None of the above

The correct answer is D:) An individual refuses to confront the person that they are angry with and instead goes to a third party. Triangulation often takes the form of venting about a problem, and it is typically seen as a very destructive practice.

133) In sociology, a triad is a

    A) Social group of three individuals
    B) Three-part analytical test
    C) Grouping of three troubling personality traits
    D) A conglomerate of three closely-placed cities
    E) None of the above

The correct answer is A:) Social group of three individuals. Triads are considered to be much more volatile than a dyad, or two-person group. However, if one of the individuals in the triad becomes dominant, then it will hold together much more tightly.

134) Changes in public policy and shifting views of women have led to

    A) Decreasing numbers of women in the workplace
    B) A glass escalator effect for women in education
    C) Increased numbers of women in sports
    D) Increased amounts of triangulation in medical fields
    E) All of the above

The correct answer is C:) Increased numbers of women in sports. Changing societal norms over the past century has led to an increased number of women in fields typically dominated by men. This includes sports, the workplace, and education.

135) The term glass escalator refers to

    A) A ceiling on the number of promotions a woman can receive in the workplace
    B) The tendency of males to do better in female-dominated fields than females in male-dominated fields
    C) Dominant individuals in a corporation preferring to have glass doors and escalators leading to their offices
    D) A continuing pattern of development throughout the world
    E) None of the above

The correct answer is B:) The tendency of males to do better in female-dominated fields than females in male-dominated fields.

136) The proportion of which of the following groups is expected to decline by 2050?

    A) Asians
    B) Hispanic
    C) Foreign-born
    D) Non-Hispanic whites
    E) All of the above

The correct answer is D:) Non-Hispanic whites. According to projections for the demographic changes in the United States over the next several decades, most ethnic groups are expected to increase whereas non-Hispanic white populations as a proportion of the total population will decrease.

137) A collective group that raises each other's children

    A) Nuclear family
    B) Blended family
    C) Extended family
    D) Kibbutz
    E) None of the above

The correct answer is D:) Kibbutz.

138) When members of the same class or group marry

    A) Endogamy
    B) Exogamy
    C) Monogamy
    D) Polygamy
    E) Polyandry

The correct answer is A:) Endogamy.

139) Which of the following statements which George Mead most likely NOT agree with?

    A) Both the elements of mind and self are products of society.
    B) People adjust their behavior according to things they see in their environments.
    C) Although personality is an inborn characteristic, it can be influenced by society.
    D) Each individual is a part of the whole society and they function in their own areas.
    E) All of the above

The correct answer is C:) Although personality is an inborn characteristic, it can be influenced by society. Mead believed that personality, or self, was completely a result of societal interactions and interpersonal communication.

140) What is it called when a group of people randomly come together to form a group?

    A) Aggregate
    B) Primary group
    C) Secondary group
    D) Census
    E) Sample

The correct answer is A:) Aggregate.

141) Folkways are

    A) The norms or expected behaviors of a society.
    B) The expected morals of a society, which are taken very seriously.
    C) Specifically enforced rules of a society.
    D) A person's general beliefs or opinions.
    E) A person's fundamental beliefs.

The correct answer is A:) The norms or expected behaviors of a society. Answer B describes mores, answer C describes laws, answer D describes attitudes, and answer E describes values.

Test Taking Strategies

Here are some test-taking strategies that are specific to this test and to other CLEP tests in general:

- Keep your eyes on the time. Pay attention to how much time you have left.
- Read the entire question and read all the answers. Many questions are not as hard to answer as they may seem. Sometimes, a difficult sounding question really only is asking you how to read an accompanying chart. Chart and graph questions are on most CLEP tests and should be an easy free point.
- If you don't know the answer immediately, the new computer-based testing lets you mark questions and come back to them later if you have time.
- Read the wording carefully. Some words can give you hints to the right answer. There are no exceptions to an answer when there are words in the question such as "always" "all" or "none." If one of the answer choices includes most or some of the right answers, but not all, then that is not the answer. Here is an example:

  The primary colors include all of the following:
  A) Red, Yellow, Blue, Green
  B) Red, Green, Yellow
  C) Red, Orange, Yellow
  D) Red, Yellow, Blue
  E) None of the above

  Although item A includes all the right answers, it also includes an incorrect answer, making it incorrect. If you didn't read it carefully, were in a hurry, or didn't know the material well, you might fall for this.
- Make a guess on a question that you do not know the answer to. There is no penalty for an incorrect answer. Eliminate the answer choices that you know are incorrect. For example, this will let your guess be a 1 in 3 chance instead.

What Your Score Means

Based on your score, you may or may not qualify for credit for your specific institution. At my campus of University of Phoenix, a score of 50 is passing for full credit. At Utah Valley State University, the score for credit is unpublished; the school will accept the credit on a case by case basis. Brigham Young University (BYU) does not accept CLEP credit. To find out what score you need for credit, you can view it online at CLEP.com but you should also verify any information with your school.

You can score between 20 and 80 on any CLEP test. Some exams include percentile ranks. Each correct answer is worth one point. You lose no points for unanswered or incorrect questions.

Test Preparation

How much you need to study depends on your knowledge of a subject area. If you are interested in literature, took it in school, or enjoy reading then your studying and preparation for the literature or humanities test will not need to be as intensive as someone who is new to literature.

This book is much different than the regular CLEP study guides. This book actually teaches you the information that you need to know to pass the test. If you are particularly interested in an area, or you want more information, do a quick search online. We've tried not to include too much depth in areas that are not as essential on the test. Everything in this book will be on the test. It is important to understand all major theories and concepts listed in the table of contents. It is also very important to know any bolded words.

Don't worry if you do not understand or know a lot about the area. With minimal study, you can complete and pass the test.

To prepare for the test, make a series of goals. Allot a certain amount of time to review the information you have already studied and to learn additional material. Take notes as you study, as it will help you learn the material.

Legal Note

References

[1] ATHERTON J S (2002) Learning and Teaching: Piaget's developmental psychology [On-line]: UK: Available: http://www.dmu.ac.uk/~jamesa/learning/piaget.htm Accessed: 28 March 2003, reprinted with permission.

[2] Kearl, Micheal C., 2003. Reprinted with permission

[3] Information for table is 2002 data taken from http://www.bartleby.com/151/a30.html

[4] Information for table is 2002 data taken from http://www.bartleby.com/151/a28.html

FLASHCARDS

This section contains flashcards for you to use to further your understanding of the material and test yourself on important concepts, names or dates. Read the term or question then flip the page over to check the answer on the back. Keep in mind that this information may not be covered in the text of the study guide. Take your time to study the flashcards, you will need to know and understand these concepts to pass the test.

Micro Sociology

Sociology Sociology

Macro Sociology

Auguste Comte

Max Weber's Social Stratification (3)

Aggregate

Primary Group

Secondary Group

Study of people and how they relate to society

Study of people in small groups

Father of Sociology

Study of large groups and entire societies

Group of people that form a group

Status, class, party

Group that shares the same goals but looser ties

A social group with intense intimacy

Social Solidarity

Social Conflict

Independent Variable

Functional Perspective

Conflict Perspective

Causation

Cross Sectional Studies

Longitudinal Studies

Unfriendly interaction
between groups

Emotional intensity of
the attachments in a
group

The idea that society is
a system

A variable the
researchers have direct
control over

One variable effects
another variable

Two elements in a
society that are in
conflict

Where people are
followed over a long
period of time

Where people of
different ages are
studied at one particular
time

Quantitative

Qualitative

Census

Sample

Case Study

Interviews

Populations

Survey

Similar in structure of
organization

The number or amount
of something

Set of cases or people
chosen from a large
group and focused on

A collection of data from
all cases or people in
the chosen set

Survey a sample
of people to gather
information

When a person along
with several others, is
studied in depth

Something mailed out
using sampling methods

People who share the
same geographic area

Mean

Mode

Median

SMSA

80/20 Rule

Four Steps of the
Scientific Method

Society

Stratification

The number that is repeated the most in a string of numbers

Average

Standard Metropolitan Statistical Area

The number in the middle of a data set

Collect data, create hypothesis, test theory, revise

80% of wealth is controlled by 20% of the people

Unequal distribution of rewards - social ladder

Group of people in an area with social ties

Classes

Upward Mobility

Downward Mobility

Status

Ascribed Status

Achieved Status

Tie

Cosmopolitan Network

An upward change in
the social system

People who share the
same position

The rank of a person in
the society

A downward change in
the social system

Position gained by
achievement

Position given but those
who do not achieve
things on their own

Network full of holes
where ties are weak

A word for a social link

Values	Folkways
Mores	Law
Culture	Role
Prejudice	Ethnocentrism

Set of manners and actions part of everyday society

Ideals about what is desirable behavior

A rule created by the government

Customs are important to the culture

Expectations of a person's behavior based on their role

Sum of all human creations

Where a person thinks their race is the best

Negative attitudes and thoughts about a particular group

Cultural Relativism

Socialization

Gender Socialization

Anti-Semitism

Anomie

Assimilation

Accommodation

Normative Order

How a person learns
how to live in their
environment

Meaning of a trait
depends on cultural
background

Prejudice of Jews

Showing the ways boys
and girls are socialized

When material is taken
in and made to fit with
existing information

Instability in culture
because of erosion of
morals

Creation of standards

The change made to
one's mind from the
process of assimilation

Merton's Anomie Theory	Looking Glass Self
Karl Marx wrote	Total Fertility Rate
Infant Mortality Rates	Demographic Transition Theory
Urban Sprawl	Durkheim's Forms of Suicide (4)

When a person's selfesteem is based how others see them

Deviance happens when people are blocked from achieving goals in legitimate ways

Amount of all children that all women could have in their childbearing years

Communist Manifesto

How populations change

Death of babies that are one year or younger

Egoistic, Altruistic, Anomic, Fatalistic

When small cities group together

Made in United States
North Haven, CT
10 December 2022

28369213R00070